Preface

The Story of Simple Things

: Arises, Exists, and Then Dies.

This book will be a book that talks about the true principles of human life and the life stages of various living things that have different life cycles. It is a book that helps summarize the story of life. It is said that there must be a moment of acceptance of what has happened and being mindful of the existence of each thing, whether large or small life or inanimate artificial things. Everything has its own cycle, so it will be explained. The story of simple things is a book to read to pass the time and to remind us that we must always be prepared for uncertainties and impermanence by living life carelessly.

An intriguing and contemplative book that delves into the deep aspects of life and existence. The exploration of various life cycles and the acceptance of impermanence are themes that can resonate with readers on a profound level. The idea of being mindful of all things, big or small, living or inanimate, and understanding their cycles adds a layer of interconnectedness to the narrative. Overall, it seems like a reflective read that encourages readers to embrace life's uncertainties and appreciate the beauty of simplicity.

Combining themes of acceptance, interconnectedness, and impermanence, "The Story of Simple Things" weaves a tapestry of introspection and contemplation. Through exploring the life stages of various living beings and even inanimate objects, the book aims to illuminate the universal cycles that govern all existence. It invites readers to reflect on the inevitability of change and the beauty found in embracing the transient nature of life.

By emphasizing the importance of mindfulness and awareness, the book encourages a deeper appreciation for the interconnected web of life that surrounds us. Whether through the growth of a plant, the flight of a bird, or the creation of artificial objects, each element plays a part in the larger story of existence. Through this lens, readers are prompted to consider their place in the vast tapestry of life and to approach each moment with a sense of gratitude and humility.

As readers immerse themselves in the pages of "The Story of Simple Things," they are invited to contemplate not only the cycles of life but also their own responses to change and uncertainty. By embracing the wisdom that comes from observing the natural world, the book serves as a gentle reminder of the beauty that can be found in simplicity and the importance of living mindfully in the present moment.

Contents

Introductions

Everything happens and is impermanent and is a cycle that will disappear.

That's a profound observation about the nature of life. Indeed, everything in life is impermanent and subject to change. Understanding the cyclic nature of things can help us appreciate the transient beauty of each moment and find peace in the midst of life's uncertainties. Embracing impermanence can also teach us to let go of attachments and practice mindfulness in the present moment.

Life is an ever-changing tapestry of experiences, emotions, and relationships. Just as the seasons change and the tides ebb and flow, we too undergo constant transformation. In this cycle of life, we experience moments of joy, sadness, growth, and loss. Embracing impermanence can help us navigate these changes with grace and acceptance.

As we reflect on the impermanent nature of life, we come to realize that clinging to things or resisting change only brings suffering. Instead, by cultivating mindfulness and living in the present moment, we can find peace and contentment amid life's flux. Every experience—whether joyful or challenging—is fleeting, a part of the ever-turning wheel of existence. With this awareness, we can approach each moment with gratitude, knowing that change is inevitable but also holds the promise of new beginnings and growth.

This reflection beautifully captures the essence of impermanence and the importance of embracing change in life. By acknowledging the transient nature of all things, we can find a deep sense of peace and acceptance. Understanding that everything is impermanent allows us to let go of attachments and appreciate each moment for what it is, without trying to hold on to it or change it.

Through mindfulness and living in the present, we can learn to ride the waves of life gracefully, knowing that change is a natural part of our existence. Every experience, whether joyful or painful, carries its own lesson and allows us to grow and evolve as individuals. By staying present and appreciating the beauty of each passing moment, we can live more fully and authentically.

In embracing impermanence, we find freedom from the anxiety and suffering that often accompany our desire for permanence and control. Instead of resisting change, we can learn to flow with life's rhythm, trusting in the wisdom of the universe and the opportunities that arise from each new phase. Ultimately, by embracing impermanence, we can find greater resilience, compassion, and joy in the ever-changing tapestry of our lives.

Exploring the theme of impermanence further, we can see how this concept extends beyond just individual experiences to encompass our relationships, possessions, and even our own sense of self. Just as the seasons transition from spring to summer to autumn, our lives go through similar cycles of growth, fruition, and eventual decline. Our relationships shift and evolve, our material possessions come and go, and our identities and beliefs transform over time.

Embracing impermanence challenges, us to let go of our attachments and expectations, allowing us to appreciate the beauty and richness of life in all its forms. It encourages us to live more fully in the present moment, savoring the fleeting joys and facing the inevitable sorrows with openness and grace. By recognizing the impermanence of everything around us, we can cultivate a deeper sense of gratitude for the precious moments we have and the connections we share with others.

Moreover, embracing impermanence can also be a source of empowerment and motivation. Knowing that change is constant, we are inspired to make the most of our time, to pursue our passions, and to take risks in the pursuit of growth and fulfillment. Rather than fearing change, we can learn to embrace it as a catalyst for personal evolution and self-discovery.

In the grand tapestry of life, impermanence weaves a thread of continuity, reminding us that as one chapter ends, another begins. It teaches us to let go of what no longer serves us, to welcome new opportunities with an open heart, and to find meaning and purpose in the ever-changing landscape of our existence. By embracing impermanence, we can navigate life's twists and turns with resilience, wisdom, and a deep sense of appreciation for the journey itself.

Indeed, the impermanence of life weaves a delicate and intricate pattern, much like the shifting seasons or the rhythmic tides. Each moment, a fleeting brushstroke on the canvas of existence, leaves its mark and then dissolves into the vastness of time.

Embracing impermanence is akin to savoring a ripe mango—the sweetness lingers on your tongue, but you know it won't last forever. The same holds true for our experiences, relationships, and emotions. They arrive, bloom, and eventually fade away, leaving behind memories etched in the fabric of our being.

Mindfulness, that gentle art of being fully present, allows us to witness life's impermanence without clinging or resisting. It's like standing on the shore, feeling the sand slip through our fingers as the waves retreat. We learn to hold joy and sorrow lightly, knowing that both are mere ripples in the grand cosmic dance.

Loss, too, is part of this intricate design. When a leaf falls from a tree, it nourishes the soil, making way for new growth. Similarly, when we bid farewell to a loved one, their essence becomes woven into our own story. We honor their memory by living fully, embracing the impermanence that binds us all.

So let us dance with impermanence, twirl in its ephemeral embrace. Let us cherish each sunrise, knowing it heralds both a beginning and an end. And when the final curtain falls, may we bow gracefully, grateful for the fleeting magic we've shared on this cosmic stage.

Chapter one

Starting with birth

Everything in this world, whether it is living things or non-living things or things created by humans or technology, begins from the beginning or birth.

Yes, everything in the world has a starting point or a beginning, whether it's living organisms like plants and animals, inanimate objects like rocks and water, or human creations like buildings and technology. The concept of birth or creation is fundamental to the existence of all things in the world. And, let's delve deeper into the concept of beginnings and birth in the context of various aspects of the world:

1. **Living Organisms**:

In the natural world, the process of birth marks the beginning of the life cycle for most organisms. From the birth of a tiny seed sprouting into a plant to the birth of a newborn animal, the cycle of life begins with this pivotal moment.

Birth is a universal phenomenon that signifies the start of growth, development, and reproduction in living organisms. It is a fundamental event that sets the stage for the various stages of life, including growth, maturation, reproduction, and eventually death. Whether it is a plant emerging from a seed or an animal coming into the world, birth is a symbol of hope, renewal, and the continuation of life's cycle.

From birth, living organisms undergo a series of stages in their life cycle that are essential for survival and propagation. As organisms grow and develop, they acquire new skills, attributes, and characteristics that enable them to adapt to their environment and fulfill their roles within their ecosystems. From infancy to adulthood, organisms experience various milestones and transformations that shape their behavior, physiology, and interactions with other species.

In the natural world, the diversity of life cycles is vast, with each species having its unique way of reproducing, growing, and aging. Some organisms undergo simple life cycles with only a few stages, while others have complex life cycles involving multiple developmental phases and reproductive strategies. Despite these variations, the underlying principle of birth marking the beginning of life remains constant across all organisms.

Birth not only initiates the life cycle but also symbolizes the resilience, tenacity, and beauty of life itself. It represents the endless possibilities and potential for growth and evolution that living organisms possess. Whether it is the emergence of a seedling breaking through the soil or the hatching of a chick from its egg, birth embodies the wonder and mystery of existence in the natural world.

2. **Non-Living Things**:

Even inanimate objects have a beginning. For instance, the formation of a crystal starts from the alignment of molecules, marking the birth of a unique structure. Similarly, the birth of a star signifies the beginning of its existence in the vast universe.

The process of birth and creation is not limited to living things alone; it extends to non-living entities as well. From the intricate formation of crystals to the majestic birth of stars, these inanimate objects also have their own stories of origin and emergence. Just like living beings, they too follow the course of creation, evolving and transforming over time. The journey of a crystal or a star from its inception to its mature state is a marvel of nature's beauty and complexity. Thus, even in the realm of non-living things, the concept of birth and beginning holds true, showcasing the wondrous diversity and interconnectedness of our universe.

With the concept of birth and creation in the non-living world, we can explore the formation of geological features like mountains, canyons, and caves. These natural formations often start with tectonic movements or erosion processes that gradually shape the Earth's surface over millions of years. The birth of a mountain range, for example, involves the collision of tectonic plates, leading to the uplift of land and the gradual creation of towering peaks.

In a similar vein, the birth of a canyon occurs through the relentless work of flowing water carving through rock layers, resulting in breathtaking gorges and ravines. The slow but persistent force of erosion gives rise to these magnificent geological wonders, each with its unique character and history.

Even man-made structures, such as buildings and bridges, have their own birth stories. The design process, construction phases, and the moment when they first come into existence mark their beginnings. From the blueprint on paper to the steel and concrete structures rising towards the sky, each step in their creation symbolizes a new chapter in their life cycle.

In essence, the concept of birth extends beyond living organisms to encompass the entire spectrum of our world, from the smallest crystal formation to the grandest mountain range. Understanding and appreciating the origin and evolution of non-living things enriches our perception of the world around us and highlights the interconnectedness of all things in the vast tapestry of existence.

3. **Human Creations**:

From works of art to scientific discoveries, human creations often start from a moment of inspiration or innovation—an intellectual birth of sorts. The birth of new ideas and technologies propels human progress and shapes the world we live in.

Throughout history, human beings have demonstrated an unparalleled ability to innovate and create. Works of art, literature, music, scientific theories, technological advancements, and social movements all stem from moments of inspiration and creativity—a spark that ignites a chain of events leading to something entirely new. These creations often reflect the values, beliefs, struggles, and aspirations of the societies that produce them, shaping our understanding of the world and ourselves.

In the realm of art, masterpieces like Leonardo da Vinci's Mona Lisa, Vincent van Gogh's Starry Night, or Shakespeare's plays have not only captured the essence of their time but have also transcended generations, inspiring countless individuals across cultures and continents.

Scientific discoveries, such as Isaac Newton's laws of motion, Albert Einstein's theory of relativity, or the decoding of the human genome, have revolutionized our understanding of the natural world and paved the way for technological innovations that have transformed how we live, work, and communicate.

Innovation and creativity are also integral to the development of technology, from the invention of the wheel and the printing press to the creation of the internet and artificial intelligence. These advancements have connected people globally, facilitated the exchange of information, and revolutionized industries, driving economic growth and societal change.

Moreover, human creations have often played a pivotal role in challenging existing norms and inspiring social progress. Movements like the civil rights movement, the feminist movement, or the LGBTQ+ rights movement have been fueled by creative expressions of resistance, solidarity, and advocacy, shaping attitudes and policies worldwide.

Overall, human creations—whether in the form of art, science, technology, or social movements—are a testament to our capacity for imagination, ingenuity, and collaboration. They reflect the best of what we are capable of achieving, serving as beacons of inspiration and catalysts for progress in an ever-changing world.

On the theme of human creations, it's important to recognize that these creations often arise from a combination of individual talent, collective effort, and cultural influences. They represent the culmination of centuries of accumulated knowledge, experimentation, and collaboration across disciplines and generations.

In the field of literature, for example, the works of authors such as Jane Austen, Fyodor Dostoevsky, or Gabriel García Márquez have not only entertained readers but have also provided profound insights into human nature, society, and the human condition. These literary creations serve as windows into different worlds and perspectives, inviting readers to explore complex emotions, dilemmas, and truths.

Similarly, in the realm of music, compositions by Bach, Beethoven, or Bob Dylan have shaped the cultural landscape and inspired countless musicians and artists. Music has the power to evoke emotions, transcend language barriers, and create connections among people from diverse backgrounds and experiences.

In the scientific domain, breakthroughs like the discovery of penicillin, the development of vaccines, or the exploration of space have revolutionized healthcare, expanded our understanding of the universe, and improved the quality of life for millions of people. These scientific creations represent the relentless pursuit of knowledge, curiosity, and the desire to push the boundaries of what is possible.

Technological innovations, from the invention of the telephone to the creation of social media platforms, have transformed the way we communicate, work, and interact with the world around us. They have democratized information, empowered individuals, and revolutionized industries, shaping the global economy and society in profound ways.

Moreover, human creations often reflect our values, beliefs, hopes, and fears. They challenge existing paradigms, provoke critical thinking, and inspire conversations about the past, present, and future. Ultimately, the intellectual birth of new ideas and technologies drives human progress, fuels innovation, and shapes the world we inhabit, reminding us of the boundless potential of the human mind and spirit.

4. **Technological Advancements**:

In the realm of technology, every innovation or invention marks a new beginning. Whether it's the birth of the internet, the first computer chip, or a breakthrough in medical science, technological advancements often redefine the way we interact with the world.

Technological advancements have greatly impacted various aspects of our lives, shaping industries, communication, healthcare, and entertainment. The birth of the internet revolutionized the way we access information and communicate globally. The development of the first computer chip laid the foundation for the digital age, leading to the creation of powerful computing devices that continue to evolve rapidly.

Breakthroughs in medical science have enabled the development of life-saving treatments, diagnostic tools, and surgical procedures, significantly improved healthcare outcomes and extending human life expectancy. Additionally, advancements in artificial intelligence, robotics, and automation are reshaping industries, enhancing productivity, and transforming the workforce.

From smartphones and social media to renewable energy and space exploration, technological advancements continue to push the boundaries of what is possible and drive innovation across all sectors. As we look to the future, the pace of technological progress shows no signs of slowing down, promising exciting opportunities and challenges ahead.

To transform the way we live, work, and interact with the world. The convergence of technologies such as big data, the Internet of Things (IoT), and machine learning is unlocking new possibilities in fields like personalized medicine, smart cities, autonomous vehicles, and sustainable energy solutions.

Artificial intelligence is revolutionizing industries by enabling autonomous systems to make decisions and perform tasks that were once limited to human capabilities. From machine learning algorithms that power recommendation systems to natural language processing tools that enable chatbots and virtual assistants, AI is driving efficiency, innovation, and new business models.

Moreover, the proliferation of connected devices and sensors is creating vast streams of data that can be analyzed in real-time to optimize processes, enhance customer experiences, and improve decision-making. The IoT ecosystem is expanding rapidly, connecting everything from wearable devices and smart appliances to industrial machinery and city infrastructure.

Renewable energy technologies, such as solar panels and wind turbines, are reshaping the global energy landscape by reducing dependence on fossil fuels and mitigating climate change. Innovations in energy storage, grid optimization, and electrification are paving the way for a more sustainable future powered by clean and renewable sources.

As we navigate the complexities of a rapidly changing technological landscape, it is essential to consider the ethical, social, and economic implications of technological advancements. Ensuring that these innovations are deployed responsibly and equitably will be critical in harnessing their full potential for the betterment of society.

5. **Cultural Evolution**: Societies and cultures also experience beginnings and births. From the birth of a nation to the inception of new traditions, cultural evolution is marked by transformative moments that shape identities and narratives.

These transformative moments often stem from a combination of external influences, internal developments, and collective actions within a society or culture. Just like individuals, societies and cultures evolve and adapt in response to changing environments, interactions with other cultures, technological advancements, and political shifts.

The birth of a nation, for example, can be a significant event in cultural evolution. It marks the foundation of a new entity with its own identity, values, and aspirations. This birth is often accompanied by the creation of symbols, rituals, and narratives that help unify the people and define their shared history and future vision.

Similarly, the inception of new traditions can also play a crucial role in cultural evolution. These traditions can emerge organically from within a society or be intentionally created to foster a sense of continuity, belonging, and meaning. Over time, these traditions may evolve, adapt, or even disappear as cultural values and practices shift.

Cultural evolution is a dynamic process marked by continuous change, innovation, and adaptation. It is shaped by a complex interplay of historical legacies, social dynamics, individual agency, and global influences. By understanding and studying these transformative moments, we can gain insights into how societies and cultures evolve over time and how they negotiate their identities in an ever-changing world.

Considering the vast tapestry of human history, we see how societies have navigated through various stages of cultural evolution, each marked by distinct milestones and turning points. From the ancient civilizations of Mesopotamia and Egypt to the rise and fall of empires like Rome and Byzantium, the story of human civilization is a testament to the enduring nature of cultural evolution.

Over time, cultures have merged, diverged, and transformed through conquests, migrations, trade, and cultural exchanges. These interactions have led to the fusion of traditions, beliefs, languages, and artistic expressions, giving rise to rich tapestries of diversity and complexity in human societies.

The birth of new artistic movements, philosophical ideas, religious beliefs, and political systems has also been instrumental in shaping cultural evolution. From the Renaissance in Europe to the Harlem Renaissance in the United States, these moments of creative and intellectual flourishing have left lasting legacies that continue to inspire and influence subsequent generations.

In the contemporary world, the forces of globalization, digital communication, and mass migration have further accelerated the pace of cultural evolution. Ideas, images, and information now travel across continents in an instant, reshaping identities, challenging norms, and fostering new forms of cultural hybridity and creativity.

As we navigate the complexities of cultural evolution in the 21st century, it becomes increasingly important to reflect on our shared histories, values, and aspirations. By recognizing the transformative moments that have shaped our societies and cultures, we can cultivate a deeper understanding of ourselves and others, fostering empathy, dialogue, and mutual respect in an interconnected world.

In essence, the idea of beginnings and births underscores the dynamic and ever-evolving nature of the world around us. Whether it's a single cell dividing to form a new life or the genesis of a groundbreaking idea, each birth symbolizes the potential for growth, change, and the continuity of existence.

Beginnings and births are symbolic of hope, renewal, and endless possibilities. They remind us that life is an ongoing journey of creation and transformation. Each new beginning is a chance to redefine ourselves, explore new horizons, and embrace the beauty of change. Just as a seed sprouts into a mighty tree or a caterpillar emerges as a butterfly, beginnings mark the genesis of endless potential and the promise of a brighter tomorrow.

The concept of beginnings and births extends beyond the physical realm into the realm of ideas and innovation. Just as a new life embodies the essence of growth and development, a groundbreaking idea represents the seed of change and progress. Innovation stems from the courage to step into the unknown, to challenge existing paradigms, and to create something entirely new. Each revolutionary idea marks a new beginning, sparking a chain reaction of inspiration and transformation that shapes the world around us. From scientific discoveries to artistic breakthroughs, these intellectual births lay the foundation for the evolution of society and culture. Therefore, by embracing beginnings and celebrating births, we honor the cyclical nature of existence and pave the way for a brighter, more vibrant future.

Things that happen in the cycle of human life

Human happiness and suffering are Things that can happen every moment and can change with time and time will be a tool for changing things around us. and it will be a cycle of arising, existing in the present, and then disappearing.

The continuous cycle of change is a fundamental aspect of life. Happiness and suffering are transient experiences that arise, exist in the present moment, and eventually fade away. Time plays a crucial role in this cycle, as it influences the ebb and flow of our experiences. Embracing the impermanence of these states can help us navigate the ups and downs of life with greater resilience and acceptance. By understanding that change is inevitable and that both joy and sorrow are fleeting, we can cultivate a deeper sense of peace and equanimity amidst life's uncertainties.

Considering the cyclical nature of life, we can appreciate that moments of happiness and suffering are not permanent states but rather fleeting experiences that come and go. Time acts as a catalyst for this continuous flux, shaping our perceptions and interactions with the world around us. By acknowledging the impermanence of our emotions and circumstances, we can develop a greater sense of mindfulness and presence in each moment.

In the grand scheme of things, the passage of time serves as a powerful force for transformation and growth. As we navigate the cycles of change in our lives, we have the opportunity to learn, evolve, and adapt to whatever comes our way. Embracing the ephemerality of both joy and sorrow can lead us to a deeper understanding of the human experience and a greater capacity for compassion, resilience, and gratitude.

By recognizing that happiness and suffering are part of the natural rhythm of life, we can cultivate a sense of balance and acceptance that allows us to ride the waves of change with grace and serenity. Time becomes not just a tool for change but a teacher that guides us through the ebbs and flows of existence, reminding us of the beauty and impermanence of all things.

This perspective encourages us to appreciate the present moment and cherish the fleeting nature of all experiences. It reminds us that nothing lasts forever and encourages us to let go of attachments and expectations that cause unnecessary suffering. Through embracing the transient nature of life, we can find a sense of freedom and peace in the midst of uncertainty and impermanence.

As we reflect on the passage of time and its transformative power, we can approach life with a sense of openness and curiosity, ready to embrace the lessons and opportunities that each moment brings. By surrendering to the natural flow of existence, we can connect more deeply with ourselves and others, fostering a sense of interconnectedness and shared humanity.

In the grand scheme of things, time serves as a gentle yet relentless force of change, nudging us towards growth, wisdom, and compassion. Embracing the temporal nature of our experiences allows us to live more fully, love more deeply, and appreciate the rich tapestry of life in all its complexity and beauty.

Reflecting on the interconnected nature of all things, we realize that our individual journeys are but threads in the larger fabric of existence. As we navigate the currents of time, we are reminded of the interplay between beginnings and endings, creation and destruction, growth and decay. Each moment holds the potential for transformation, offering us the chance to shed old skins, release outdated beliefs, and step into new ways of being.

In the dance of impermanence, we find both solace and challenge. We are invited to embrace the uncertainty that accompanies change, to welcome the unknown with open arms, and to trust in the wisdom of the unfolding present. Like the seasons that come and go, we are called to honor the cyclical nature of life, appreciating the gifts of each phase while letting go with grace when it is time to move on.

As we surrender to the flow of time, we discover a sense of resilience that allows us to weather life's storms, a capacity for compassion that enables us to empathize with others' struggles, and a deep well of gratitude that springs forth from the recognition of life's preciousness. Time, in its inexorable march, becomes not an enemy to resist but a friend to embrace—an ever-present companion on our journey of self-discovery and growth.

May we learn to dwell in the beauty of each passing moment, to savor the sweetness of joy and the richness of sorrow, and to walk with faith and courage as we continue to unfold along the path of our becoming. And may we always remember that in the grand scheme of things, time is not our master but our guide, leading us ever onward towards the fullness of our own potential and the boundless expanse of our shared humanity.

After the birth of a child There is both suffering and happiness. Suffering begins with the birth of man and it Followed since birth until death. Happiness, on the other hand, is also present throughout life, mingling with the suffering in various forms and moments. The coexistence of suffering and happiness is an inherent part of the human experience, shaping our perspectives, emotions, and interactions with the world around us.

Suffering and joy are intertwined in the intricate tapestry of existence. The journey of life is a delicate balance between moments of pain and moments of pleasure. It is through our experiences of suffering that we can truly appreciate the beauty of joy, and it is through our moments of happiness that we can find solace in the face of hardship. These contrasting emotions shape us, mold us, and ultimately, define the essence of our humanity. In the end, it is the ebb and flow of suffering and happiness that give depth and richness to the complex fabric of life.

The impermanence of life

Contemplating the impermanence of life and the cycles of change, both joy and suffering, can lead us to reflect on the nature of existence and the choices we make. It is crucial to train ourselves to cultivate awareness and mindfulness in navigating these ups and downs. By developing a perspective system that guides us to learn and observe our consciousness, we can better understand our responses to life's challenges and joys. This reflective practice can help us make conscious decisions that lead to personal growth, compassion, and inner peace. Ultimately, the direction in which we choose to train ourselves is pivotal in shaping our experiences and our interactions with the world around us.

To explore and deepen your understanding of the complexities of life's transient nature. Embracing impermanence can be the key to unlocking profound insights into the human experience. By acknowledging the inevitability of change and the dualities of joy and suffering, we can learn to appreciate the beauty in each moment, even amidst challenges.

Training ourselves to be present and conscious in our lives involves cultivating practices like mindfulness, meditation, self-reflection, and gratitude. These tools can help us navigate the uncertainties of life with resilience and grace. By developing a perspective system that encourages learning and observation, we can gain clarity on our values, beliefs, and intentions, allowing us to make choices that align with our true selves.

As we embark on this journey of self-discovery and growth, it's essential to remember that life is a continuous process of evolution and learning. Embracing change and striving for personal development can lead to a more meaningful and fulfilling existence. By choosing to train ourselves in a direction that fosters awareness, compassion, and authenticity, we empower ourselves to create a life that is rich in purpose and connection.

These reflections offer profound insights into the essence of embracing impermanence and navigating life's uncertainties with grace and resilience. By acknowledging the transient nature of existence and the inherent dualities of joy and suffering, we can cultivate a deeper understanding of the human experience and appreciate the beauty inherent in each moment.

Practices such as mindfulness, meditation, self-reflection, and gratitude serve as invaluable tools to help us stay present and conscious in our daily lives. Through these practices, we can develop a heightened sense of awareness, enabling us to navigate life's challenges with a sense of clarity and purpose. By aligning our choices and actions with our core values and beliefs, we can live authentically and in harmony with our true selves.

As we embark on a journey of self-discovery and personal growth, it is important to recognize that change is a natural part of life. Embracing this continuous process of evolution allows us to embrace new opportunities for learning and development, leading to a more meaningful and fulfilling existence. By fostering awareness, compassion, and authenticity within ourselves, we can create a life that is rich in purpose and connection, ultimately empowering us to live more intentionally and fully.

Embracing impermanence and the transient nature of life can be a profound source of growth and wisdom. It encourages us to let go of attachment to outcomes and embrace the ebb and flow of life's inevitable changes. By acknowledging the impermanence of all things, we can learn to appreciate and savor the present moment, recognizing that each experience, whether joyful or challenging, is a fleeting part of our journey.

In our pursuit of mindfulness and self-awareness, we cultivate a deeper connection with ourselves and the world around us. Through practices like meditation and reflection, we can develop the ability to observe our thoughts and emotions with compassion and non-judgment, fostering a greater sense of inner peace and resilience. These practices help us build a foundation of emotional intelligence, enabling us to respond to life's ups and downs with grace and equanimity.

Gratitude is another powerful tool that can transform our perspective and enhance our well-being. By cultivating a daily practice of gratitude, we shift our focus from what is lacking to what we already have, fostering a sense of abundance and contentment. Gratitude opens our hearts to the beauty and blessings present in our lives, even during times of difficulty, reminding us of the preciousness of each moment.

As we navigate the complexities of life, it is essential to approach our journey with a spirit of curiosity and openness. By embracing change and personal growth as integral parts of our evolution, we empower ourselves to learn, adapt, and evolve into the best versions of ourselves. Through self-discovery, introspection, and a commitment to lifelong learning, we can embark on a transformative path towards greater self-awareness, fulfillment, and connection with the world around us.

These are wise words that highlight the importance of gratitude, self-discovery, and openness in our lives. Practicing gratitude allows us to appreciate the present moment and shift our perspective towards abundance. Embracing change and personal growth as essential components of our journey enables us to evolve and reach our full potential. By fostering self-awareness and a commitment to learning, we can deepen our connection with ourselves and the world, leading to greater fulfillment and understanding.

Cultivating an attitude of gratitude can be a powerful daily practice that enriches our lives in numerous ways. It allows us to acknowledge and appreciate the simple joys and blessings that often go unnoticed in the busyness of daily life. By taking a moment each day to reflect on what we are grateful for, we can cultivate a positive outlook, cultivate resilience, and enhance our overall well-being. Gratitude has the transformative power to shift our focus from what is lacking to what is abundant, fostering a sense of contentment and fulfillment.

In addition to gratitude, approaching life with a sense of curiosity and openness can lead to greater personal growth and transformation. When we embrace change as a natural part of our journey and remain open to new experiences, we create opportunities for learning, self-discovery, and growth. This mindset encourages us to step out of our comfort zones, challenge ourselves, and explore new possibilities that can lead to deeper connections and a richer, more fulfilling life.

By engaging in self-discovery through practices such as introspection, mindfulness, and journaling, we can gain valuable insights into our thoughts, emotions, and behaviors. This process of self-exploration helps us uncover our strengths, identify areas for growth, and cultivate greater self-awareness. With a deeper understanding of ourselves, we can make more informed choices, set meaningful goals, and align our actions with our values and priorities.

Furthermore, a commitment to lifelong learning empowers us to expand our knowledge, skills, and perspectives throughout our lives. Whether through formal education, reading, attending workshops, or engaging in conversations with others, the pursuit of learning keeps our minds active, curious, and open to new ideas. By continuously seeking out opportunities to learn and grow, we not only enrich our own lives but also contribute positively to the world around us.

In conclusion, by practicing gratitude, embracing change, fostering self-discovery, and committing to lifelong learning, we can embark on a transformative journey towards greater self-awareness, fulfillment, and connection with ourselves and the world. These practices serve as pillars for personal growth and well-being, guiding us along a path of continuous evolution and discovery.

The birth or giving birth of a new thing, be it a human being or any invention. After emerging into this world, there must be an origin of life and the spirit of these things.

Whether it be the birth of a new human being or the invention of something novel. The notion of origin and the spirit imbued in these creations are indeed fascinating aspects to explore. Is there a particular angle or perspective you are interested in discussing further regarding these themes?

Along the lines of creation and emergence, one can reflect on the profound symbolism present in the act of giving birth or bringing forth new creations. Whether it's the miracle of a new life entering the world or the innovative spark of a new invention, there is an undeniable sense of awe and wonder in witnessing something new come into existence.

This act of creation often carries with it a deep sense of purpose and meaning. The birthing process, whether literal or metaphorical, symbolizes growth, evolution, and the relentless cycle of life. It represents a journey from the conceptual stage to tangible reality, wherein the creator infuses a part of themselves into their creation, thereby imparting a unique essence and spirit to it.

Furthermore, the origin of life and the spirit embodied in these creations evoke questions about our place in the universe and the interconnectedness of all things. It prompts contemplation on the nature of existence, the power of intention, and the profound impact that our creations can have on the world around us.

Ultimately, the act of giving birth to new life or ideas serves as a reminder of the beauty and complexity of the world we inhabit, urging us to cherish the creative potential within us and to nurture the spirit that drives us to bring new things into being.

Reflecting on the origin of life and the profound interconnectedness of all things can lead to a deep sense of awe and wonder about our existence. It raises questions about the mysteries of the universe, our purpose within it, and the power of creation that resides within each of us.

Contemplating the nature of existence and the impact of our creations can inspire us to approach life with intention and mindfulness. It encourages us to recognize the intrinsic value of our creative abilities and the transformative influence they can have on the world around us.

By embracing our role as creators and nurturers of life and ideas, we acknowledge the responsibility that comes with such power. We are reminded of the need to cultivate empathy, compassion, and wisdom in our endeavors, ensuring that our creations contribute positively to the interconnected web of existence we are part of.

In harnessing our creative potential and honoring the spirit of creation that resides within us, we not only enrich our own lives but also contribute to the greater tapestry of life in ways that resonate with beauty, harmony, and purpose.

Reflecting on the origins of life and the intricate interconnectedness of the universe can inspire a sense of humility and reverence for the sheer vastness and complexity of existence. It prompts us to contemplate our place in the grand scheme of things and the significance of our actions in shaping the world around us.

As we ponder the mysteries of life and creation, we may find ourselves grappling with existential questions about the nature of reality, the origin of consciousness, and the underlying forces that govern the cosmos. This exploration can lead to a deeper appreciation for the beauty and wonder that abound in the world, as well as a greater sense of interconnectedness with all living beings.

When we recognize the power of intention and the impact of our creative endeavors, we are called to approach our work with mindfulness, purpose, and a deep sense of responsibility. We understand that our creations have the potential to shape the world for better or for worse, and we strive to imbue them with meaning, integrity, and compassion.

By honoring the creative spark within us and nurturing the spirit of innovation and exploration, we tap into a wellspring of inspiration that fuels our quest for discovery and self-expression. We become conscious co-creators of our reality, actively shaping our experiences and leaving our mark on the tapestry of existence.

In embracing our role as stewards of life and guardians of the creative flame, we affirm our connection to the larger ecosystem of being and acknowledge the profound influence we have on the world around us. Through our acts of creation, big and small, we contribute to the ongoing process of evolution and transformation, enriching not only our own lives but also the lives of others in ways that ripple across time and space.

Linking the life cycle at birth

Life that arises on this planet, including our own solar system, is a building material that is the starting point for various things, stars, and the origins of the human world and the solar system. The universe has cycles of stars and stars. Including humans on this earth are part of the cycle.

The reflection on the interconnectedness of life on Earth with the broader cosmic cycles in the universe. Life on our planet, including humans, is indeed built upon the elements originating from stars and the processes of star formation and evolution. We are all interconnected and part of the grand cycles of the cosmos. It's fascinating to think about how we are linked to the vastness of the universe through these cosmic processes.

Let's explore this concept further. The formation of elements within stars through processes like fusion and stellar evolution is fundamental to the creation of the building blocks of life. These elements are then dispersed through the universe via supernovae explosions and other cosmic events, eventually coming together to form planets, like Earth, where life can emerge and evolve.

Humans, as part of this intricate web of existence, have the unique capacity to reflect on our place in the cosmos and ponder the very forces that shaped us. By studying the stars, galaxies, and the universe at large, we gain insights into our origins and the cyclical nature of creation and destruction that governs the cosmic tapestry.

As we journey through this cosmic dance, it is a humbling reminder of our connection to the universe and the interwoven nature of all things. Each of us, in our own way, is a part of this grand narrative, contributing to the ongoing evolution of the cosmos and the continuous cycles of life and rebirth that define our existence.

Our shared existence with all living beings on this planet, and our interconnectedness with the vast universe beyond, underscores the importance of embracing humility and compassion in our interactions with each other and the world around us. Through contemplation of the cosmos, we can cultivate a deeper appreciation for the beauty and complexity of existence and find inspiration to live in harmony with the rhythms of nature and the mysteries of the universe.

As we navigate our way through the mysteries of the cosmos, let us remember that we are but a small part of a vast and wondrous whole. Let us approach each day with a sense of wonder and gratitude, knowing that we are all united in our shared journey through the cosmos.

Contemplating the vastness of the cosmos and the intricate connections that bind us to it can evoke a sense of awe and wonder that transcends our individual existence. It is through this recognition of our place in the grand tapestry of the universe that we can find solace in times of uncertainty and inspiration in moments of reflection.

In the grand scheme of things, our lives are but fleeting moments in the expanse of time and space. However, within these fleeting moments lie opportunities for growth, connection, and transformation. As we gaze up at the night sky and ponder the mysteries of the cosmos, we are reminded of the inherent beauty and resilience of life itself.

May we approach each day with a sense of reverence for the interconnectedness of all things and a deep appreciation for the wonders of the universe. Let us embrace our role as stewards of this precious planet and co-creators of the cosmic dance, knowing that our actions ripple out beyond ourselves and contribute to the ever-unfolding story of creation.

Beautifully said! Our lives are indeed filled with opportunities for growth and connection, and the mysteries of the cosmos serve as a powerful reminder of the beauty and wonder that surrounds us. By approaching each day with reverence and appreciation for the interconnectedness of all things, we can truly embrace our role as stewards of our planet and active participants in the cosmic dance. Our actions, no matter how small, have the power to create ripples of change that contribute to the ongoing story of creation. Let us nurture this sense of connection and responsibility as we navigate the vast expanse of existence, seeking to leave a positive impact on the world around us.

To contemplate the vastness of the universe, we are humbled by our place in the grand tapestry of existence. Each moment, each interaction, each decision we make holds the potential to shape not only our own lives but the lives of others and the world at large. It is a profound responsibility and a tremendous privilege to be able to contribute to the ongoing evolution of our shared reality.

As we journey through the cosmos on this tiny blue planet, let us remember that we are all interconnected, bound together by the threads of time and space. Our individual stories are but chapters in the larger narrative of humanity, and our collective actions have the power to influence the course of history. With this awareness, let us strive to act with compassion, empathy, and integrity, knowing that our choices can reverberate far beyond our immediate circle of existence.

In the face of uncertainty and adversity, let us draw strength from the resilience of life itself and the enduring spirit of creation. Like stars shining in the night sky, let our light illuminate the darkness and inspire others to embrace the beauty and potential that resides within each of us. And as we continue to journey through the boundless expanse of time and space, may we carry with us a sense of wonder, gratitude, and reverence for the interconnected web of life that unites us all.

Chapter Two

Have identity and determination.

After birth, human beings are raised and grown until they have the ability to take care of themselves, leading a stable life, having an identity, having skills, having a career, and living in the present.

It's true that after birth, human beings go through a process of growth and development that involves acquiring various skills, forming an identity, and eventually becoming self-sufficient individuals capable of taking care of themselves. This journey includes gaining education, developing social and emotional skills, and finding a career path that suits their interests and abilities. Ultimately, humans strive to live fulfilling lives in the present moment, continually learning and growing along the way.

Here the various stages of human development:

1. **Infancy and Early Childhood**:

In the early stages of life, infants rely heavily on their caregivers for survival. They learn to trust and communicate, laying the foundation for future relationships and emotional well-being.

These early interactions are crucial for the infant's socio-emotional development. Through bonding with their caregivers, infants learn to regulate their emotions, develop a sense of security, and form attachments that will shape their relationships later in life. Caregivers who respond consistently and sensitively to their infant's needs help foster a secure attachment, which can have long-lasting positive effects on the child's emotional and social development.

While caregivers play a vital role in shaping a child's emotional well-being, early relationships with peers and other family members also contribute to a child's social development. As children grow, they begin to interact with a wider circle of individuals, learning valuable social skills such as cooperation, empathy, and conflict resolution. Positive experiences in these interactions can further support a child's emotional development and help them navigate the complexities of relationships as they mature.

It is essential for caregivers and other significant individuals in a child's life to provide a supportive and nurturing environment that encourages healthy emotional development. By fostering trust, open communication, and a sense of security, adults can help children build the foundation for strong and meaningful relationships throughout their lives. Early experiences with caregivers and peers can significantly impact a child's emotional well-being, laying the groundwork for resilience, empathy, and positive social connections in the years to come.

Nurturing positive social relationships during childhood lays the foundation for healthy emotional development in adulthood. Through interactions with caregivers, peers, and family members, children learn to navigate complex social situations, manage emotions, and build connections with others. These early experiences shape their understanding of themselves and the world around them, influencing their ability to form healthy relationships later in life.

Caregivers play a crucial role in modeling positive social behaviors and teaching children's essential skills for building and maintaining relationships. By providing a safe and nurturing environment where children can express themselves and learn from their interactions, caregivers help them develop social competence and emotional resilience. It is important for caregivers to be attentive and responsive to children's emotional needs, offering support and guidance as they navigate social interactions. Encouraging empathy, teaching conflict resolution skills, and fostering a sense of belonging can help children develop strong social bonds and a deep sense of emotional well-being.

By recognizing the significance of early social experiences in shaping emotional development, caregivers and other significant individuals can create a supportive environment that promotes positive social interactions and sets the stage for healthy relationships throughout a child's life.

Building strong social connections during childhood is essential for overall well-being and long-term success. Children who have positive early relationships with caregivers, peers, and family members are more likely to develop important social and emotional skills that serve as the building blocks for healthy relationships in adulthood. Caregivers play a fundamental role in fostering emotional intelligence and social competence in children. By providing love, support, and guidance, caregivers help children learn to regulate their emotions, communicate effectively, and develop a sense of empathy and compassion for others. These essential skills enable children to form meaningful relationships and navigate the complexities of social interactions throughout their lives.

In addition to caregivers, peers and other family members also play a critical role in shaping a child's social development. Interactions with peers provide children with opportunities to practice cooperation, negotiation, and perspective-taking, helping them learn how to work collaboratively with others and resolve conflicts peacefully. Positive experiences with family members, such as siblings, grandparents, aunts, and uncles, can also contribute to a child's emotional well-being by providing additional sources of support, love, and connection.

As children grow and interact with a broader social circle, they continue to learn and refine their social skills, such as active listening, problem-solving, and emotional regulation. These skills are crucial for building and maintaining healthy relationships in adolescence and adulthood, as they empower individuals to communicate effectively, understand others' perspectives, and navigate social challenges with confidence and resilience.

By recognizing the importance of early social relationships in shaping emotional development, caregivers and other significant individuals can create a nurturing environment that supports children in building strong social connections and thriving emotionally. Investing in children's social and emotional well-being from an early age not only benefits them in the present but also lays the groundwork for fulfilling and meaningful relationships in the future.

Indeed, acknowledging the crucial role of early social relationships in emotional development highlights the significance of providing children with a supportive and caring environment. Caregivers and other influential figures play a vital role in fostering these connections, as they can model healthy behaviors, teach empathy, and provide emotional support that is essential for a child's development. By prioritizing children's social and emotional well-being, we can help them develop resilience, empathy, and strong relationship skills that will serve them throughout their lives. The investment in nurturing children's emotional and social development early on not only benefits the children themselves but also contributes to the creation of a more compassionate and connected society as they grow into adults.

Emotional development begins in infancy and continues through childhood, adolescence, and into adulthood. Early social relationships, particularly with caregivers, create the foundation for how individuals learn to regulate their emotions, form attachments, empathize with others, and navigate social interactions. Positive and secure relationships in early childhood have been linked to better emotional regulation, higher self-esteem, and improved mental health outcomes later in life.

Caregivers and other significant individuals can support children's emotional development by being responsive, nurturing, and creating a safe and supportive environment where children feel valued and understood. By providing consistent love, attention, and guidance, caregivers help children develop a secure attachment style that forms the basis for healthy relationships in the future.

Encouraging children to express their emotions, teaching them coping strategies, and helping them understand and manage their feelings are all important aspects of fostering emotional well-being. By actively engaging with children's emotions, caregivers can help them develop emotional intelligence, empathy, and effective communication skills that are essential for building strong social connections.

Investing in children's social and emotional development not only enhances their well-being in the present but also equips them with the tools they need to navigate a complex and interconnected world. By prioritizing emotional resilience, empathy, and positive relationship-building skills from an early age, we can empower children to lead fulfilling lives and contribute positively to their communities.

2. **Childhood and Adolescence**:

During childhood and adolescence, individuals develop cognitive abilities, social skills, and a sense of self-identity. They attend school, participate in various activities, and acquire knowledge and experiences that shape their worldview.

These formative years are crucial for building the foundation of a person's personality and future development. Through interactions with family, peers, teachers, and other authority figures, individuals learn valuable life skills such as communication, problem-solving, empathy, and critical thinking. They also start forming their values, beliefs, and goals, which will influence their decisions and actions later in life.

Furthermore, childhood and adolescence are periods of rapid brain development, characterized by significant changes in cognitive functions like memory, reasoning, and decision-making. As young individuals navigate through different challenges and experiences, they adapt and grow, developing resilience, perseverance, and emotional intelligence.

Overall, the journey through childhood and adolescence is a dynamic process of self-discovery, learning, and growth that lays the groundwork for the individual's future relationships, achievements, and overall well-being.

And expand further on the topic.

During childhood and adolescence, individuals not only develop cognitive abilities and social skills but also undergo significant emotional and physical changes. These developmental stages are marked by exploration, curiosity, and a search for identity and purpose. Adolescents often grapple with questions about their place in the world, their strengths and weaknesses, and their aspirations for the future.

School plays a crucial role during these formative years, providing structured learning environments where children and teenagers acquire academic knowledge, socialize with peers, and engage in extracurricular activities that foster creativity and teamwork. Educators and mentors guide students in their learning journey, helping them build confidence, resilience, and a growth mindset.

Moreover, family dynamics and relationships with parents and siblings have a profound impact on a child's development. Supportive and nurturing family environments contribute to emotional stability and self-esteem, while conflicts or challenging family situations can affect a child's well-being and behavior.

As individuals progress through childhood and adolescence, they gradually refine their values, beliefs, and personal interests, shaping their unique identity. This process is influenced by cultural, societal, and environmental factors, as well as personal experiences and interactions with others.

In essence, the journey from childhood to adolescence is a complex and transformative period of growth and self-discovery that sets the stage for a person's future relationships, achievements, and overall well-being.

During this developmental journey, individuals may explore different paths, question their beliefs, and seek new experiences to better understand themselves and the world around them. They may also face challenges and obstacles that require resilience and adaptability to navigate successfully.

Family, peers, teachers, and other significant figures play crucial roles in supporting and guiding individuals as they navigate this period of growth and self-discovery. Their influence, along with societal norms and cultural expectations, can shape an individual's values, attitudes, and aspirations.

Ultimately, the transition from childhood to adolescence is a time of both vulnerability and opportunity, where individuals have the chance to explore their identity, discover their strengths and weaknesses, and lay the foundation for their future. Embracing this period of growth with openness, curiosity, and a willingness to learn can lead to a deeper understanding of oneself and a stronger sense of purpose and direction in life.

As individuals progress through this journey of self-discovery, they are also likely to encounter new interests, skills, and passions that shape their identity. Whether through academic pursuits, extracurricular activities, volunteer work, or personal hobbies, adolescents often explore various avenues to better understand their unique talents and strengths. These experiences not only contribute to personal growth but also help individuals build confidence, resilience, and a sense of purpose.

Moreover, as adolescents interact with diverse social groups and engage in conversations about important issues, they begin to form their own perspectives and beliefs about the world. Exposure to different cultures, backgrounds, and viewpoints can foster empathy, tolerance, and a broader understanding of social issues, ultimately shaping their values and attitudes.

Throughout this transformative period, individuals may also face challenges such as peer pressure, academic stress, identity crises, or societal expectations. Overcoming these obstacles requires self-reflection, emotional intelligence, and a strong support system to navigate successfully.

In essence, the journey from childhood to adolescence is a dynamic and multifaceted process of self-discovery, growth, and personal development. By embracing the opportunities for exploration, learning, and reflection that this period presents, individuals can lay a solid foundation for their future and cultivate a strong sense of identity and purpose.

Indeed, the transition from childhood to adolescence is a crucial phase in an individual's life, marked by significant changes and challenges. Navigating this transformative period requires a combination of self-awareness, emotional resilience, and the ability to adapt to new situations. Developing a strong sense of identity and purpose during this time is essential for building confidence and resilience in the face of peer pressure, academic stress, and societal expectations.

Self-reflection plays a key role in helping individuals understand their values, interests, and aspirations.

By taking the time to introspect and evaluate their beliefs and goals, young people can gain clarity about who they are and what they want to achieve. This process of self-discovery is essential for building a strong foundation for personal growth and development.

Emotional intelligence, which encompasses skills such as self-awareness, self-regulation, empathy, and social skills, is also crucial during this period of transition. Developing emotional intelligence allows individuals to navigate complex social dynamics, manage stress effectively, and build healthy relationships with others. By honing these skills, young people can better understand and express their emotions, make informed decisions, and cultivate resilience in the face of challenges.

A strong support system consisting of family, friends, teachers, mentors, and other positive influences is another key factor in helping individuals overcome obstacles and thrive during this period of change. Having a network of supportive individuals who listen, provide guidance, and offer encouragement can make a significant difference in a young person's ability to navigate the challenges of adolescence and emerge stronger and more resilient.

By embracing the opportunities for growth and self-discovery that adolescence offers, individuals can lay a solid foundation for their future and build the confidence and skills needed to navigate life's challenges with resilience and purpose. This dynamic and multifaceted journey of personal development is essential for building a strong sense of identity, purpose, and well-being as young people transition from childhood to adulthood.

This transformative journey requires individuals to cultivate a growth mindset and a willingness to learn from both successes and setbacks. Embracing a growth mindset means viewing challenges as opportunities for growth, believing in one's ability to learn and improve, and maintaining a positive attitude even in the face of adversity. By adopting this perspective, young people can develop resilience, perseverance, and a sense of agency that empowers them to overcome obstacles and reach their full potential.

Exploration and curiosity are also essential components of the journey from childhood to adolescence. Encouraging individuals to explore a variety of interests, pursue new hobbies, and engage in diverse experiences can help them discover their passions, talents, and values. This process of exploration allows young people to broaden their horizons, expand their perspectives, and develop a deeper understanding of themselves and the world around them.

Furthermore, fostering a sense of empathy and compassion towards others is crucial for building strong relationships and creating a positive impact on the community. By understanding and respecting the perspectives, feelings, and experiences of others, individuals can cultivate meaningful connections, build trust, and contribute to a more inclusive and supportive social environment. Developing empathy also enables young people to navigate conflicts constructively, communicate effectively, and collaborate with others towards common goals.

In conclusion, the journey from childhood to adolescence is a transformative period of self-discovery, growth, and personal development that requires self-reflection, emotional intelligence, and a supportive environment. By embracing the opportunities for exploration, learning, and growth that this phase presents, individuals can build a strong foundation for their future, cultivate a sense of identity and purpose, and navigate life's challenges with resilience, empathy, and a growth mindset. This dynamic and multifaceted process of personal development is essential for shaping young people into confident, compassionate, and capable individuals who are ready to take on the opportunities and challenges that lie ahead.

3. **Young Adulthood**:

In young adulthood, individuals typically pursue higher education, establish careers, and form intimate relationships. This period is characterized by personal growth, independence, and exploration of one's values and goals.

During young adulthood, individuals often undergo significant changes in various aspects of their lives. They may transition from being dependent on their families to taking on more responsibilities, such as managing their finances, living independently, and making important life decisions. This stage of life also presents opportunities for self-discovery, as individuals may explore different interests, hobbies, and career paths to find what truly resonates with them.

Higher education plays a crucial role during this stage, as it provides opportunities for specialized knowledge and skill development that can lead to career advancement. Many young adults pursue further education beyond high school to equip themselves with the necessary qualifications for their chosen professions. Establishing a career is also a key focus during young adulthood, as individuals begin to build their professional identity, gain work experience, and strive for advancement in their chosen fields.

Additionally, forming intimate relationships is a significant aspect of young adulthood. This stage often involves exploring romantic and platonic relationships, developing communication and conflict resolution skills, and forming long-lasting connections with others. Building relationships can contribute to emotional growth, provide a support system during challenging times, and help individuals develop a sense of belonging and connection.

Overall, young adulthood is a dynamic and transformative period characterized by a range of experiences that contribute to personal growth, self-discovery, and the establishment of a foundation for future success and fulfillment.

Young adulthood is also a time for individuals to start defining their values, beliefs, and aspirations. It is a period marked by introspection and exploration, where young adults may question societal norms, challenge their own assumptions, and seek to align their actions with their core values. This process of self-discovery can lead to a greater sense of self-awareness and authenticity, allowing individuals to make decisions that are more in line with their true selves.

Furthermore, young adulthood often involves navigating various transitions and challenges, such as moving to a new city, starting a new job, or experiencing changes in relationships. These experiences can be both exhilarating and daunting, requiring individuals to adapt to new environments, learn new skills, and overcome obstacles along the way. Developing resilience, problem-solving skills, and the ability to cope with uncertainty are essential during this stage of life.

It's worth noting that young adulthood is not a one-size-fits-all experience. Individuals may have diverse backgrounds, goals, and challenges that shape their unique journey through this period. Some may pursue unconventional paths, take risks, or prioritize personal growth over conventional markers of success. Understanding and respecting these differences can help create a more inclusive and supportive environment for all young adults as they navigate this transformative stage of life.

Navigating the complexities of young adulthood requires a combination of self-discovery, openness to new experiences, and a willingness to learn from both successes and setbacks. Building a strong support network of friends, mentors, and resources can also be invaluable in providing guidance and encouragement along the way. By embracing the opportunities for growth and self-improvement that young adulthood offers, individuals can set the foundation for a fulfilling and purposeful life journey.

Exploring avenues for personal and professional development is a key aspect of young adulthood. This phase often involves making important decisions about education, career paths, relationships, and personal values. Taking the time to reflect on one's strengths, interests, and ambitions can help individuals make informed choices that align with their passions and long-term goals.

Moreover, embracing a growth mindset can be particularly beneficial during this stage. Viewing challenges as opportunities for learning and growth can foster resilience and perseverance in the face of obstacles. It's important to remember that setbacks are a natural part of the journey and can provide valuable insights that contribute to personal development and self-improvement.

Cultivating a sense of curiosity and a willingness to explore diverse perspectives and experiences can also enrich one's understanding of the world and foster empathy and compassion for others. Engaging with different cultures, engaging in community service, or pursuing creative outlets can broaden one's horizons and deepen their appreciation for the richness and diversity of human experience.

Ultimately, young adulthood is a time of immense possibility and potential for transformation. By approaching this stage with curiosity, resilience, and an open mind, individuals can embark on a journey of self-discovery and growth that lays the groundwork for a meaningful and fulfilling life ahead.

During this phase of life, individuals often have the freedom to explore different paths, establish their identity, and cultivate their values and beliefs. It is a time for making choices that shape their future, whether it's related to education, career, relationships, or personal development. By embracing curiosity, young adults can seek new experiences, learn from challenges, and broaden their perspectives.

Resilience plays a crucial role in navigating the inevitable ups and downs of this period. It empowers individuals to bounce back from setbacks, adapt to changes, and persist in pursuing their goals. Developing resilience allows young adults to withstand adversity, manage stress, and continue growing even in the face of difficulties.

Approaching young adulthood with an open mind fosters a willingness to embrace diverse perspectives, challenge assumptions, and welcome new opportunities for learning and personal change. It encourages individuals to question their beliefs, expand their horizons, and engage with the world in a more empathetic and inclusive way.

By cultivating curiosity, resilience, and an open mind, young adults can lay a strong foundation for personal growth and fulfillment. This transformative period offers a unique chance to discover one's passions, strengths, and values, setting the stage for a purposeful and meaningful life journey ahead.

Young adulthood is a time of both excitement and uncertainty, as individuals navigate the complexities of adult life while still exploring their own identities and aspirations. It is a phase marked by significant transitions, whether it be moving away from home, starting a career, building relationships, or discovering one's purpose in the world.

Embracing curiosity during this time means being open to new experiences, ideas, and perspectives. It involves asking questions, seeking knowledge, and stepping out of one's comfort zone to explore the endless possibilities that lie ahead. Curiosity fuels personal growth and development, enabling young adults to find their passions, interests, and values as they carve out their own path in life.

Resilience is another vital quality that serves as a pillar of strength during the challenges and obstacles that inevitably arise in young adulthood. It involves bouncing back from setbacks, learning from failures, and developing the inner fortitude to persevere in the face of adversity. Resilience empowers individuals to weather life's storms with grace and determination, emerging stronger and more capable of surmounting future challenges.

An open mind is a powerful tool for growth and transformation during young adulthood. Being open to new possibilities, different perspectives, and diverse experiences allows individuals to expand their horizons, challenge their assumptions, and cultivate empathy and understanding for others. An open mind fosters a sense of curiosity and a willingness to engage with the world in all its complexity, setting the stage for continuous learning and personal evolution.

In conclusion, young adulthood is a time ripe with potential for self-discovery, growth, and transformation. By embracing curiosity, resilience, and an open mind, individuals can embark on a journey of exploration and empowerment that shapes their future trajectory and sets the stage for a fulfilling and meaningful life ahead.

Indeed, young adulthood is a pivotal phase in one's life journey where opportunities for personal development and self-realization abound. Embracing curiosity paves the way for new experiences and learning, while resilience enables individuals to navigate challenges with strength and determination. An open mind allows for flexibility and adaptability in the face of change, fostering growth and transformation. By seizing the potential of this transformative period, individuals can lay a strong foundation for a future filled with purpose and fulfillment.

to invest in relationships, both personal and professional, as these connections can provide support, guidance, and valuable insights. Developing strong communication skills can enhance interpersonal dynamics and empower individuals to express themselves effectively.

Moreover, prioritizing self-care and well-being is crucial during young adulthood. Establishing healthy habits, such as regular exercise, nutritious eating, and sufficient rest, can bolster physical and mental health. Additionally, cultivating mindfulness practices or engaging in activities that bring joy and relaxation can promote emotional balance and overall wellness.

Setting goals and working towards them with dedication can instill a sense of purpose and accomplishment. Whether pursuing higher education, embarking on a new career path, or pursuing creative endeavors, having clear objectives can drive motivation and focus. Embracing opportunities for personal and professional development, such as seeking mentorship, acquiring new skills, or stepping out of comfort zones, can foster growth and expand horizons.

In essence, young adulthood is a time of immense possibility and potential for individuals to shape their identities, forge meaningful connections, and lay the groundwork for a fulfilling future. By embracing curiosity, resilience, and an open mind, individuals can navigate the complexities of this transformative phase with confidence and optimism, setting the stage for a rich and rewarding life journey ahead.

During this critical period of young adulthood, individuals are often faced with important decisions related to their education, career, relationships, and personal growth. By cultivating a sense of curiosity, young adults can explore various paths and opportunities, allowing them to discover their passions and interests. This curiosity fuels a thirst for knowledge and new experiences, enabling individuals to broaden their perspectives and deepen their understanding of themselves and the world around them.

Additionally, resilience plays a vital role in navigating the inevitable challenges and setbacks that come with this stage of life. By developing resilience, individuals can bounce back from setbacks, adapt to changes, and persevere in the face of adversity. This ability to weather storms and learn from failures is essential for personal growth and building strength in character.

An open mind is also crucial during young adulthood, as it allows individuals to embrace diversity, consider different viewpoints, and welcome new opportunities for growth and development. By keeping an open mind, young adults can break free from limitations, biases, and preconceived notions, enabling them to explore new possibilities and make informed decisions that align with their values and aspirations.

Ultimately, by embodying curiosity, resilience, and an open mind, young adults can navigate the complexities of this transformative phase with grace and confidence. These qualities serve as powerful tools for self-discovery, personal growth, and laying the foundation for a fulfilling and purposeful future. By embracing these attributes, individuals can harness their full potential, forge meaningful connections with others, and embark on a journey of lifelong learning and self-fulfillment.

On this journey of self-discovery and growth, young adults can also benefit greatly from seeking out mentorship and guidance from experienced individuals in their chosen fields or areas of interest. Mentors can offer valuable insights, advice, and support, helping young adults navigate challenges, make informed decisions, and unlock their full potential. By fostering mentorship relationships, individuals can learn from the wisdom and experiences of others, accelerating their personal and professional growth and gaining invaluable perspectives that can guide them on their path forward.

Furthermore, cultivating a strong sense of community and building meaningful connections with peers and mentors can provide a support system that nurtures personal well-being and resilience. By surrounding themselves with like-minded individuals who share their values and goals, young adults can form a strong network of support, encouragement, and collaboration. These connections can offer not only emotional support but also opportunities for collaboration, learning, and mutual growth.

In addition to seeking out mentorship and building a strong community, young adults can also benefit from honing their emotional intelligence and communication skills. Developing the ability to understand and manage their emotions, empathize with others, and communicate effectively can enhance their relationships, decision-making abilities, and overall well-being. By practicing emotional intelligence and effective communication, individuals can navigate interpersonal dynamics, resolve conflicts constructively, and build strong and meaningful relationships that enrich their lives.

In essence, young adulthood is a time of immense growth, exploration, and self-discovery. By embracing curiosity, resilience, an open mind, seeking mentorship, building a supportive community, and honing their emotional intelligence and communication skills, individuals can navigate this transformative phase with confidence, grace, and optimism. Through these efforts, young adults can lay the foundation for a fulfilling and purposeful future, setting themselves on a path towards a rich and rewarding life journey ahead.

4. **Middle Adulthood**:

Middle adulthood is a time of stability and

productivity, often marked by career advancement, family-building, and a focus on long-term goals. Individuals may reassess their priorities and make decisions that align with their values.

During middle adulthood, people typically have accumulated a wealth of experience and knowledge that they can apply to their work and personal lives. This can lead to increased confidence and a sense of fulfillment as they strive to achieve their goals. Additionally, relationships with partners, children, and extended family members may become more central as individuals establish strong social connections and support networks. Overall, middle adulthood is a period of growth and development where individuals often find themselves balancing various aspects of their lives to create a sense of stability and satisfaction.

Middle adulthood is also a time when individuals may begin to confront aging-related concerns, such as health issues and financial planning for retirement.

This stage often prompts reflection on past choices and future aspirations, leading many to consider how they want to spend their later years. Some may also experience a renewed sense of purpose and a desire to give back to their community or engage in activities that bring them joy and fulfillment. In essence, middle adulthood is a phase of life characterized by a combination of growth, introspection, and preparation for the future, as individuals navigate the complexities of balancing work, family, and personal well-being.

These years also commonly entail adjustment to changes in family dynamics, such as children leaving home or becoming more independent, as well as potentially caring for aging parents. The challenges and opportunities that come with middle adulthood can vary greatly from person to person, influenced by factors like career satisfaction, relationship status, health, and overall life circumstances. It is a time when individuals may reassess their values, goals, and priorities, and make important decisions that can shape the trajectory of their later years. Despite the potential stressors and uncertainties that may arise during this period, middle adulthood also offers many opportunities for personal growth, self-discovery, and building meaningful connections with others. By embracing this stage of life with resilience, openness, and a willingness to adapt, individuals can not only navigate its challenges effectively but also cultivate a sense of fulfillment and well-being as they move forward in their journey.

Middle adulthood, typically ranging from around age 40 to 65, is a crucial period in the developmental journey of individuals. It serves as a bridge between the youthful vigor and exploration of earlier years and the reflective wisdom and contentment often associated with later life stages. Some key developmental tasks during this phase include establishing a sense of generativity, which involves contributing to society and leaving a positive legacy for future generations, as well as achieving a sense of integrity by reconciling past experiences and forming a coherent identity.

One of the central themes of middle adulthood is the concept of generativity versus stagnation, as proposed by psychologist Erik Erikson. Generativity refers to the desire to nurture and guide the next generation, whether through raising children, mentoring younger individuals, or contributing to the community in meaningful ways. This impulse to create a lasting impact and make a difference can be a powerful motivator during this stage, driving individuals to seek opportunities for personal and social growth.

Moreover, middle adulthood is often a time of reflection on one's accomplishments and failures, relationships, and personal growth trajectories. It may involve reevaluating career choices, pursuing new interests or hobbies, and cultivating deeper connections with loved ones. Many individuals also grapple with the reality of their own mortality and strive to make the most of their remaining years by focusing on activities and relationships that bring them joy and fulfillment.

In terms of physical and cognitive changes, middle adulthood is marked by a gradual decline in physical strength and agility, as well as changes in cognitive abilities such as processing speed and memory. However, these changes are often offset by a wealth of life experience, emotional maturity, and problem-solving skills honed over the years. With age comes a greater capacity for emotional regulation, empathy, and perspective-taking, qualities that can enhance interpersonal relationships and lead to a deeper sense of connection with others.

Overall, middle adulthood is a period of significant growth, self-discovery, and transition, where individuals grapple with existential questions, explore new possibilities, and lay the groundwork for a fulfilling and meaningful later life. By embracing the challenges and opportunities that come with this stage, individuals can cultivate resilience, wisdom, and a sense of purpose that can sustain them through the inevitable ups and downs of the aging process.

During middle adulthood, individuals may also experience changes in their social roles, such as becoming parents, taking on more responsibilities at work, caring for aging parents, or transitioning to new career paths. These transitions can bring both fulfillment and stress as individuals navigate their multiple roles and obligations.

Maintaining physical health through regular exercise, balanced nutrition, and adequate rest becomes increasingly important during middle adulthood to support overall well-being. Engaging in activities that promote mental stimulation, such as learning new skills or pursuing hobbies, can also help offset cognitive changes and enhance brain function.

It's essential for individuals in middle adulthood to prioritize self-care, seek social support, and cultivate healthy coping mechanisms to navigate the challenges of this life stage. Developing a sense of acceptance for the aging process and being open to seeking guidance from mental health professionals or support groups can also aid in managing the emotional complexities that may arise.

Ultimately, middle adulthood offers a unique opportunity for personal growth, introspection, and reevaluation of priorities. By embracing the changes and opportunities that come with this stage of life, individuals can navigate the complexities of aging with grace, resilience, and a sense of purpose.

Exploring and adapting to changes in relationships is also a significant aspect of middle adulthood. Friends may come and go, family dynamics shift, and romantic relationships evolve. Nurturing meaningful connections with loved ones, developing effective communication skills, and practicing empathy and understanding can help navigate the complexities of interpersonal relationships during this stage of life.

Career satisfaction and financial stability often take on heightened importance during middle adulthood. Some individuals may consider making significant career changes, pursuing further education, or focusing on professional development to align their work with their values and goals. Financial planning and preparing for retirement become key considerations as individuals look towards the future.

Middle adulthood is also a time when individuals may reevaluate their life goals, values, and beliefs. Reflecting on past experiences, setting new objectives, and seeking personal fulfillment become integral to shaping a sense of purpose and direction. Engaging in activities that bring joy, fulfillment, and a sense of accomplishment can contribute to overall well-being and satisfaction during this life stage.

Additionally, middle adulthood often presentations opportunities for individuals to contribute to their communities, mentor younger generations, and engage in volunteer work or philanthropic endeavors. Giving back to society and leaving a positive legacy can provide a sense of fulfillment and connection to something greater than oneself.

In summary, middle adulthood is a dynamic and transformative period that offers a unique blend of challenges and opportunities for personal growth and self-discovery. By embracing change, nurturing relationships, pursuing personal goals, and maintaining physical and mental well-being, individuals can navigate this stage of life with resilience, purpose, and a sense of fulfillment.

Middle adulthood presents individuals with a variety of opportunities for personal growth and fulfillment. Engaging in community contributions, mentoring others, volunteering, and participating in philanthropic endeavors are ways to make a positive impact on society and leave a lasting legacy. These activities not only benefit others but also provide a sense of purpose and connection to something greater than oneself.

In summary, middle adulthood is a period of transformation and growth where individuals can navigate challenges and seize opportunities for personal development. By embracing change, nurturing relationships, pursuing personal goals, and maintaining physical and mental well-being, people can find resilience, purpose, and fulfillment during this stage of life.

In middle adulthood, individuals often face a variety of unique challenges that can lead to personal growth and self-discovery. For many, this period represents a time of reflection and reevaluation of priorities, leading to a deeper understanding of themselves and their place in the world. As responsibilities may shift, such as raising children, caring for aging parents, or advancing in a career, individuals are compelled to adapt and evolve in response to new circumstances.

Moreover, middle adulthood is an opportune time for individuals to focus on their well-being, both physically and mentally. Prioritizing healthy lifestyle choices, such as regular exercise, proper nutrition, and stress management, can contribute to maintaining overall wellness and vitality. Additionally, seeking support from mental health professionals or engaging in activities that promote emotional well-being, such as mindfulness practices or therapy, can aid in navigating the complex emotions and challenges that may arise during this stage of life.

Furthermore, building and nurturing meaningful relationships with family, friends, and community members is essential for well-being and satisfaction in middle adulthood. Strong social connections provide a support system during times of need, offer opportunities for companionship and shared experiences, and contribute to a sense of belonging and connection. Investing time and effort in cultivating these relationships can lead to greater emotional resilience and fulfillment throughout this stage of life.

Overall, middle adulthood is a time of significant personal growth and exploration. By embracing the challenges and opportunities that come with this stage of life, individuals can create a foundation for resilience, purpose, and fulfillment that will support them as they continue to navigate the journey of aging and self-discovery.

5. **Later Adulthood**:

In later adulthood, individuals may experience retirement, reflection on their life achievements, and a focus on maintaining physical and mental well-being. Relationships with family and community become increasingly important during this stage.

During later adulthood, individuals may also find themselves with more free time to pursue hobbies, interests, and leisure activities that they may not have had time for earlier in life. Travel, volunteering, spending time with grandchildren, and other activities can bring fulfillment and joy during this stage. It's also common for older adults to face challenges such as managing chronic health conditions, adapting to changes in their social networks, and coping with the loss of loved ones. Developing coping strategies, staying socially connected, and seeking support when needed can all contribute to a sense of well-being and fulfillment in later adulthood.

As individuals navigate later adulthood, they may also grapple with existential questions about the meaning and purpose of their lives. Reflecting on past experiences, accomplishments, and missed opportunities can be a part of this introspective process. Some individuals may seek to leave a legacy through mentorship, philanthropy, or other forms of contribution to society. Maintaining cognitive abilities through activities like puzzles, games, and lifelong learning can also be important for promoting mental well-being in later life. Overall, this stage of life presents a unique opportunity for personal growth, connection with others, and finding meaning in one's life journey.

It's important to recognize that later adulthood can be a time of reflection and exploration of existential questions. Individuals may ponder the meaning of their lives, assess their accomplishments, and consider their impact on the world. Engaging in activities that stimulate cognitive abilities, such as puzzles and learning, can help maintain mental sharpness and overall well-being.

Many people in later adulthood also seek to leave a legacy, whether through mentoring younger generations, contributing to charitable causes, or pursuing other forms of social impact. This desire to create a lasting impact can bring a sense of fulfillment and purpose to this stage of life.

Ultimately, navigating later adulthood involves a mix of introspection, connection with others, and personal growth. By embracing these aspects, individuals can find meaning and fulfillment as they continue their life journey.

Exploring existential questions in later adulthood can lead individuals to delve deeper into their values, beliefs, and life purpose. This introspective process often involves reflecting on past experiences, relationships, and personal growth. Some individuals may find solace and meaning in connecting with their spirituality or engaging in practices such as meditation or mindfulness to cultivate a sense of inner peace and fulfillment.

Maintaining social connections and engaging in activities that foster a sense of community and belonging are also crucial aspects of well-being in later life. Building and nurturing relationships with family, friends, and peers can provide support, companionship, and a sense of belonging that enriches one's life experiences.

Embracing new challenges, hobbies, or passions can also be rewarding in later adulthood, as they offer opportunities for personal growth, creativity, and self-expression. Whether it's learning a new skill, pursuing a long-held interest, or embarking on new adventures, these endeavors can add vibrancy and fulfillment to this stage of life.

Ultimately, navigating the complexities of later adulthood involves a delicate balance of self-reflection, social engagement, personal development, and embracing new experiences. By approaching this stage of life with curiosity, openness, and a willingness to explore new horizons, individuals can cultivate a sense of purpose, connection, and vitality that enriches their later years.

Navigating the complexities of later adulthood requires a nuanced approach that intertwines self-reflection, social engagement, personal growth, and a willingness to embrace new experiences. By fostering curiosity, openness, and a desire to explore uncharted territories, individuals can infuse their later years with purpose, connection, and vitality, thus making this stage of life fulfilling and enriching. Living fully in later adulthood necessitates a multifaceted strategy that incorporates various elements such as introspection, community involvement, continuous personal evolution, and a readiness to step out of one's comfort zone. By maintaining a sense of wonder, staying receptive to new possibilities, and actively seeking novel experiences, individuals can infuse their later years with meaning, interconnectedness, and a vibrant energy that sustains and uplifts them. This holistic approach enables them to navigate the intricate landscape of aging with resilience, authenticity, and a renewed zest for life.

Through these stages of development, human beings navigate various challenges, learn valuable life skills, and evolve as individuals with unique identities and aspirations. It's a continuous journey of growth and self-discovery that shapes one's character and contributes to a fulfilling life.

Indeed, the journey of human development is a profound and multifaceted process that encompasses physical, cognitive, emotional, and social growth. From infancy to old age, individuals encounter hurdles, triumphs, setbacks, and achievements that all contribute to their overall personal development. This journey involves acquiring new knowledge, honing skills, forming relationships, overcoming obstacles, and adapting to changing circumstances. Each stage presents its own set of challenges and opportunities for growth, helping individuals develop a sense of resilience, independence, empathy, and self-awareness. Ultimately, this continuous process of growth and self-discovery is essential for building a strong foundation for a meaningful and fulfilling life.

Understanding the various stages of human development, such as infancy, childhood, adolescence, adulthood, and old age, provides insight into the unique challenges and opportunities individuals face at different points in their lives. In each stage, individuals cultivate essential life skills, such as resilience, problem-solving, decision-making, emotional regulation, and interpersonal communication. These skills are developed through experiences, interactions with others, exposure to diverse perspectives, and the ability to adapt to new situations.

As individuals progress through life, they shape their identities, values, beliefs, and aspirations based on their experiences and personal growth. This journey of self-discovery and personal development is not always linear or straightforward, as it involves facing uncertainties, making difficult choices, and navigating complex relationships. Nonetheless, overcoming obstacles and learning from past experiences contribute to personal growth and character development.

Moreover, human development is not only influenced by internal factors but also by external factors such as family, culture, society, education, and environment. These external influences shape individuals' perspectives, beliefs, behaviors, and aspirations, further adding complexity to the process of personal growth and self-discovery. In essence, human development is a dynamic and continuous journey marked by growth, learning, and transformation. Embracing this journey with openness, curiosity, resilience, and a willingness to evolve can lead to a deeper understanding of oneself, a stronger sense of purpose, and a more fulfilling life rich in experiences and connections with others.

Human development is a multifaceted process that is influenced by a variety of factors, both internal and external. Internal factors such as genetics, temperament, and cognitive abilities play a crucial role in shaping individuals from an early age. However, external factors such as family dynamics, cultural background, societal norms, educational opportunities, and environmental conditions also significantly impact an individual's development throughout their life.

Family, as the primary socializing agent, plays a fundamental role in shaping a person's values, beliefs, and social behaviors. A supportive and nurturing family environment can foster a sense of security and self-esteem, contributing positively to one's overall development. Conversely, adverse family dynamics or experiences can hinder optimal development and lead to challenges in emotional and psychological well-being.

Culture and society also play a vital role in human development by providing individuals with a framework of norms, values, and expectations that guide their behaviors and interactions with others. Cultural influences shape our identity, social relationships, and worldview, influencing our choices and shaping our perceptions of the world around us.

Education is another critical external factor that significantly impacts human development. Access to quality education can enhance cognitive abilities, critical thinking skills, and knowledge acquisition, empowering individuals to reach their full potential and contribute meaningfully to society. On the other hand, disparities in educational opportunities can perpetuate social inequalities and limit individuals' prospects for personal growth and success.

Environmental factors, such as access to healthcare, safe living conditions, and exposure to toxins or pollutants, also play a crucial role in human development. The physical environment in which individuals live can impact their health, well-being, and overall quality of life, influencing their developmental outcomes and future opportunities.

Overall, human development is a complex interplay between internal and external factors that shape individuals' growth and evolution over time. By understanding and appreciating the multifaceted influences on human development, we can cultivate a more holistic approach to personal growth and self-discovery, fostering resilience, adaptability, and a deeper sense of connection with ourselves and the world around us.

Understanding the intricate web of internal and external factors that contribute to human development requires a nuanced and comprehensive perspective. Each individual's life journey is unique, shaped by a combination of genetic predispositions, early life experiences, social interactions, and environmental influences. These factors interact in complex ways to mold personality traits, cognitive abilities, emotional responses, and social behaviors, ultimately defining who we are and who we become.

Family dynamics, in particular, play a pivotal role in laying the foundation for human development. From early childhood through adolescence and beyond, families serve as the primary source of emotional support, socialization, and identity formation. Parenting styles, family structure, communication patterns, and the quality of relationships within the family unit profoundly influence individuals' self-concept, interpersonal skills, and psychological well-being.

Cultural and societal influences further shape human development by providing norms, values, and traditions that guide individuals' thoughts, beliefs, and behaviors. Culture defines our sense of identity, belonging, and purpose, shaping our understanding of the world and influencing our decisions and actions. Societal structures, such as institutions, social hierarchies, and economic systems, also play a crucial role in shaping opportunities, constraints, and power dynamics that impact human development at both individual and collective levels.

Education plays a transformative role in human development by equipping individuals with knowledge, skills, and competencies that empower them to navigate the complexities of the modern world. Quality education fosters intellectual growth, critical thinking, creativity, and lifelong learning, enabling individuals to adapt to change, solve problems, and contribute meaningfully to society. Moreover, education can serve as a vehicle for social mobility, empowering individuals to overcome barriers and achieve their full potential.

The physical environment in which individuals live also significantly influences human development. Access to clean air, water, nutritious food, healthcare services, and safe living conditions plays a critical role in promoting physical health, cognitive development, and overall well-being. Environmental factors such as pollution, climate change, natural disasters, and urbanization can pose significant challenges to human development, affecting individuals' health, quality of life, and future prospects.

In conclusion, human development is a multifaceted and dynamic process shaped by a complex interplay of internal and external factors. By recognizing and understanding the diverse influences that impact our growth and self-discovery, we can cultivate a more holistic and compassionate approach to personal development, fostering resilience, empathy, and a deeper sense of connection with ourselves and the world around us.

Chapter Three

Everything in this world is impermanent and will part according to day and time.

The statement you provided reflects the Buddhist concept of impermanence, which teaches that all things in the world are transient and subject to change. Understanding impermanence can help people cultivate mindfulness, appreciate the present moment, and find peace amidst the inevitable changes of life.

Yes, the concept of impermanence is a key teaching in Buddhism, emphasizing the ever-changing nature of existence. By recognizing impermanence, individuals can free themselves from attachment to things that are temporary and fleeting, leading to a deeper sense of acceptance and inner peace. Embracing impermanence can also help individuals navigate life's challenges with greater resilience and flexibility.

With the theme of impermanence in Buddhism, the concept extends beyond the physical realm to include emotional states, relationships, and even our sense of self. By understanding that all things are impermanent, individuals can learn to let go of past grievances, release attachment to future outcomes, and focus on living fully in the present moment. This practice of mindfulness enables one to appreciate the beauty and richness of each passing experience without being consumed by desires or fears about the future. Ultimately, embracing impermanence can lead to a deeper sense of interconnectedness with all beings and a profound realization of the ever-changing nature of reality.

Buddhism teaches that impermanence is not something to be feared or resisted but rather embraced as a fundamental aspect of life. By accepting impermanence, individuals can cultivate a sense of equanimity and freedom from suffering. The practice of impermanence encourages individuals to develop qualities such as patience, adaptability, and non-attachment, which can greatly enhance their overall well-being and spiritual growth.

Through meditation and mindfulness practices, individuals can deepen their understanding of impermanence and integrate this wisdom into their daily lives. By observing the impermanent nature of thoughts, emotions, and sensations without clinging or aversion, one can develop a sense of inner peace and tranquility. This shift in perspective helps individuals to live more authentically and respond to the challenges of life with greater wisdom and compassion.

In essence, the concept of impermanence in Buddhism serves as a powerful reminder of the interconnectedness of all things and the transient nature of existence. By embracing impermanence as a natural part of life, individuals can cultivate a deeper sense of acceptance, gratitude, and presence, leading to a more meaningful and fulfilling life journey.

Embracing impermanence in Buddhism also brings about a profound shift in perspective towards material possessions and worldly pursuits. By recognizing the impermanent nature of material wealth and external success, individuals can reduce their attachment to these transient pleasures and instead focus on cultivating inner qualities such as generosity, kindness, and compassion. This change in attitude can lead to a greater sense of contentment and fulfillment, as one learns to derive true happiness from within rather than relying on external conditions for satisfaction.

Moreover, the practice of impermanence in Buddhism encourages individuals to let go of rigid ideas of self and identity. By understanding that the self is also impermanent and ever-changing, individuals can transcend the limitations of ego and cultivate a deeper sense of interconnectedness with all beings. This realization opens the door to greater empathy, compassion, and understanding towards others, fostering harmonious relationships and a more compassionate society.

In essence, by embracing impermanence in all aspects of life, individuals can embark on a profound spiritual journey towards inner peace, wisdom, and liberation. The practice of impermanence serves as a powerful reminder to live mindfully, appreciate the present moment, and cultivate a deep sense of gratitude for the beauty and richness of life's ever-changing tapestry. By incorporating the teachings of impermanence into daily life, one can navigate life's ups and downs with grace and resilience, ultimately leading to a more fulfilling and enriching existence.

Birth, old age, illness and death are normal things.

Yes, birth, old age, illness, and death are universal experiences that are a natural part of the human life cycle. Each stage brings its own challenges and opportunities for growth and learning. Embracing the full spectrum of life experiences can help us appreciate the preciousness of life and develop a deeper understanding of our own mortality.

Our journey through life is marked by various stages and experiences. Birth, with its promise of new beginnings, heralds the start of our existence, full of potential and possibilities. As we grow older, we navigate the complexities of relationships, education, and career, shaping our identities and values along the way.

As time advances, we inevitably face the realities of old age, where physical and mental faculties may weaken, offering opportunities for reflection and wisdom. Illness, be it temporary or chronic, reminds us of our vulnerability and the importance of caring for our bodies and minds.

Ultimately, death, the great equalizer, looms as the inevitable conclusion to our earthly journey. While it may evoke fear and sorrow, it also underscores the transient nature of life and the importance of living with purpose and gratitude.

In accepting the natural cycle of birth, old age, illness, and death, we can cultivate a deeper appreciation for the rich tapestry of human existence and find meaning in the transient beauty of our shared journey.

Contemplating death can serve as a powerful motivator to live authentically, to cherish the present moment, and to nurture meaningful connections with others. By embracing our mortality, we can reevaluate our priorities, pursue our passions wholeheartedly, and strive to leave a positive impact on the world around us.

Rather than viewing death as a source of existential dread, we can choose to see it as a reminder of our interconnectedness and a catalyst for personal growth. Through this perspective, we can approach life with a sense of purpose and seize the opportunity to shape our legacy through acts of kindness, creativity, and compassion.

In the face of life's impermanence, let us strive to make each day meaningful, to savor the beauty of existence, and to embrace the full spectrum of human experience with courage and grace to contemplate the intricacies of life allows us to navigate our journey with a sense of curiosity and wonder. By acknowledging the cyclical nature of existence, we can find solace in the idea that our individual stories are but threads woven into the larger tapestry of humanity.

As we confront the reality of our mortality, we are reminded of the preciousness of time and the opportunity it presents to make a positive impact on the world. Each moment becomes an invitation to express gratitude, show love, and seek growth in the face of life's inevitable uncertainties.

In the midst of life's challenges and joys, we can find strength in our shared humanity and in the collective resilience that arises from facing the unknown together. It is through this shared experience that we can find meaning, cultivate compassion, and discover the beauty that exists in the midst of life's impermanence.

Embracing the transient nature of our earthly existence can be a profound act of courage and liberation, freeing us to live authentically, love deeply, and create a legacy that extends beyond our individual lifetimes. In accepting the inevitability of death, we awaken to the beauty of the present moment and the transformative power of living with purpose and gratitude.

Life is an experiences with various

Life is a journey filled with various experiences, both positive and negative, that shape individuals and contribute to their personal development. From the innocence and wonder of childhood to the challenges and responsibilities of adulthood, each stage of life offers opportunities for learning, growth, and self-discovery.

Throughout this journey, individuals navigate through ups and downs, facing triumphs and setbacks that influence their perspectives, beliefs, and behaviors. These experiences help individuals build resilience, empathy, and wisdom as they adapt to different circumstances and overcome obstacles.

As individuals age and mature, they undergo significant transformations in their beliefs, goals, and priorities, leading to a continuous cycle of growth and renewal. Reflecting on past experiences, learning from mistakes, and embracing new challenges are all integral parts of this cycle of rebirth, allowing individuals to evolve, improve, and find deeper meaning in their lives.

Ultimately, the cycle of rebirth is a reminder that life is a continuous journey of self-discovery and growth, where every experience, whether positive or negative, contributes to the ongoing process of personal transformation and renewal.

This concept of the cycle of rebirth can be understood as a metaphorical journey of self-discovery and growth that individuals go through as they navigate the various stages of life. Just like the changing seasons or the cycle of birth and death in nature, humans also experience cycles of growth, renewal, and transformation.

As individuals age and accumulate experiences, they often reassess their beliefs, values, and priorities in light of new information and insights gained along the way. This process of reflection and introspection can lead to a deeper understanding of oneself and one's place in the world, fostering personal growth and development.

Learning from past mistakes and setbacks is an essential part of this cycle, as it allows individuals to make adjustments, course corrections, and improvements in their lives. Embracing new challenges and stepping out of one's comfort zone can also be catalysts for personal growth and transformation, leading to greater resilience, adaptability, and self-awareness.

Ultimately, the cycle of rebirth serves as a reminder that change is inherent in the fabric of life and that each experience, no matter how challenging or rewarding, holds the potential for growth and renewal. By embracing this process of self-discovery and evolution, individuals can cultivate a sense of purpose, fulfillment, and meaning in their lives, creating a rich tapestry of experiences that contribute to their personal and spiritual growth.

Continuing on the theme of the cycle of rebirth, it's important to acknowledge that personal transformation is not always a linear process. Just as nature goes through cycles of growth, decay, and renewal, individuals too may experience periods of stagnation, uncertainty, or setbacks before undergoing a profound transformation.

During times of struggle or challenges, individuals may find themselves questioning their beliefs, values, and identity. These moments of introspection and self-examination can be catalysts for growth, as they force individuals to confront their fears, vulnerabilities, and limitations, ultimately leading to a deeper understanding of oneself and the world around them.

Moreover, the cycle of rebirth is not limited to individual growth but can also be observed in the context of relationships, careers, and personal endeavors. Just as individuals evolve and change over time, so too do their relationships, goals, and aspirations. Embracing change, adapting to new circumstances, and letting go of the past are all essential aspects of this ongoing process of renewal and transformation.

In essence, the cycle of rebirth underscores the dynamic nature of life, highlighting the constant ebb and flow of experiences, emotions, and challenges that shape our journey of self-discovery and growth. By embracing change, learning from past experiences, and cultivating a mindset of curiosity and resilience, individuals can navigate this cycle with grace and wisdom, ultimately emerging stronger, wiser, and more self-aware.

It's important to acknowledge the inevitability of aging and death as part of the natural cycle of life. As humans, we experience various stages of life, from birth to old age, and eventually, death. While the deterioration of the body with age is a natural process, it can also bring challenges such as illnesses and diseases. Understanding and accepting this cycle can help us appreciate the preciousness of life and make the most of our time here.

To explore the complexities of aging and mortality can lead us to reflect on our own lives and relationships. As we witness the passage of time and the changes that come with it, we may find ourselves contemplating the legacy we wish to leave behind and the impact we have had on others. It is through these reflections that we can find meaning and purpose in the face of life's impermanence.

While the physical body may deteriorate with age, it is essential to remember that our spirit and essence are enduring. The wisdom we gain over the years, the memories we create, and the love we share continue to shape our legacy long after we are gone. Embracing the journey of life in all its stages, including old age and death, can lead to a deeper appreciation of the interconnectedness of all living beings and a greater sense of gratitude for the gift of existence.

In confronting the realities of human mortality, we are reminded of the fragility of life and the importance of living authentically and with integrity. By acknowledging our own impermanence, we are encouraged to live each moment fully, cherishing the experiences and relationships that bring richness and meaning to our lives. Ultimately, the cycle of life serves as a poignant reminder of the interconnectedness of all living beings and the profound beauty of existence in all its transient glory.

In this episode, we will talk about the end of human life, old age, illness, disease, or the body that keeps getting older and until death comes. That is, the cycle of life in which the body is impermanent, born, grown, and the world moves on. Then he decayed and died because his body grew old and finally became a corpse.

Reflecting on the impermanence of life is a deeply profound and universal aspect of human existence. The inevitability of aging, illness, and death underscores the transient nature of our physical bodies and serves as a poignant reminder of the preciousness of every moment we have. Embracing this cycle of life allows us to cultivate a deeper appreciation for the interconnectedness of all living beings and the beauty that exists in the ebb and flow of existence.

As we witness the aging process and the eventual decline of the physical body, we are invited to contemplate the legacy we wish to leave behind and the impact we have had on the world around us. By living authentically and with integrity, we can strive to make the most of our time here, fostering meaningful connections and nurturing a sense of purpose that transcends our mortal limitations.

In acknowledging our own impermanence, we are compelled to confront the fundamental questions of existence and the legacy we wish to create. By embracing the cycle of life with grace and acceptance, we can find solace in the knowledge that our time here is a gift to be cherished and shared with others, leaving a lasting imprint of love and compassion on the world we leave behind.

Embracing the reality of impermanence can be a transformative experience, challenging us to reevaluate our priorities and find deeper meaning in our lives. As we journey through the stages of life, from birth to old age and ultimately death, we are confronted with the fragility of our physical existence and the fleeting nature of time. This awareness can inspire us to live more intentionally, savoring each moment and embracing the richness of human experience.

In the face of mortality, we are called to confront our fears and anxieties, seeking wisdom and insight in the inevitable passage of time. It is through this process of introspection and acceptance that we can find a sense of peace and wholeness, recognizing the intrinsic beauty of our own impermanence and the interconnectedness of all beings.

The cycle of life reminds us of the intricate web of relationships that bind us together, transcending individual boundaries and weaving a tapestry of shared humanity. In honoring this interconnectedness, we can cultivate compassion, empathy, and gratitude for the journey we all share, finding solace in the knowledge that we are not alone in our struggle to make sense of the mystery of existence.

As we navigate the complexities of life and death, may we find comfort in the transient nature of our physical forms, embracing the ebb and flow of existence with grace and resilience. By acknowledging our impermanence, we can learn to live more fully, love more deeply, and appreciate the profound beauty of each moment we are given.

Embracing the impermanence of life allows us to release attachment to the material and transient, focusing instead on nurturing connections that endure beyond the confines of time and space. Through acts of kindness, understanding, and forgiveness, we can mend the frayed threads of our shared humanity and strengthen the bonds that unite us in our collective journey.

In this ever-evolving tapestry of existence, may we find the courage to confront our fears, the wisdom to embrace change, and the resilience to weather life's inevitable storms with grace and humility. Let us walk this path together, supporting and uplifting one another as we navigate the intricate dance of birth, growth, decay, and renewal that defines our intertwined destinies.

As we reflect on the interconnectedness of all beings and the sacredness of each moment, may we approach life with an open heart and a spirit of reverence, honoring the interconnected web that sustains us all. In this way, we can find solace in the beauty of our shared journey and draw strength from the knowledge that we are all interconnected in the vast tapestry of life.

As we gaze upon the breathtaking complexity of the natural world and the intricate relationships that define our existence, we are reminded of the profound interconnectedness that binds us together in a delicate dance of existence. Every living being, every breath taken, every heartbeat resonates within the intricate tapestry of life, weaving a narrative of shared experiences and mutual dependencies that transcend individual boundaries.

In our quest for understanding and meaning, we are called to embrace the exquisite fragility of life, to cherish the fleeting moments of joy and sorrow, and to honor the interconnected threads that unite us in our collective journey. Like a symphony of diverse voices harmonizing in unity, we are each a unique note contributing to the ever-evolving composition of existence.

Through the gentle art of mindfulness and presence, we can attune ourselves to the subtle rhythms of the universe, recognizing the beauty in moments of stillness and the wisdom inherent in transitions of birth and rebirth. In this tapestry of existence, we find both solace and inspiration, for it is within the interplay of light and shadow, growth and decay, that the true essence of life reveals itself in all its radiant complexity.

Let us continue to honor the interconnected web of life that sustains us, nurturing compassion, empathy, and gratitude as guiding principles on our shared journey. In embracing the cycles of creation and destruction, in witnessing the symphony of life unfold in its myriad forms, may we find meaning, purpose, and belonging in the vast interconnectedness of all things.

From the two parts mentioned above, it will be about birth and living. as in the present, but firmly in the period of life, and this third part will be about illness and aging of the human body. This is a matter of nature that occurs during human time.

Sure, let's discuss the third part about illness and aging of the human body. As we progress through life, our bodies undergo various changes. Aging is a natural process that involves the gradual decline in bodily functions and the emergence of age-related illnesses.

With aging, our bodies may become more susceptible to illnesses such as cardiovascular diseases, arthritis, Alzheimer's disease, cancer, and other chronic conditions. The immune system also tends to weaken with age, making older adults more vulnerable to infections.

Additionally, aging is often accompanied by physical changes such as decreased muscle mass and bone density, reduced skin elasticity, and a decline in senses like vision and hearing. Cognitive functions may also decline, leading to memory problems and decreased mental sharpness.

While aging and illness are inevitable parts of life, it's essential to take care of our physical and mental health through regular exercise, healthy eating, proper rest, and engaging in activities that stimulate the mind. Seeking medical care and staying informed about age-related health issues can help in managing and potentially delaying the onset of illnesses associated with aging.

Using regular health check-ups and screenings can aid in early detection of potential health issues, allowing for timely intervention and treatment. Maintaining social connections and engaging in activities that bring joy and fulfillment can also contribute to overall well-being in our later years.

However, it's important to acknowledge that despite our best efforts, aging and illness are natural processes that come with their own challenges. Coping with the physical and emotional changes that accompany aging can be difficult, and it's normal to experience feelings of loss, vulnerability, and uncertainty.

As individuals navigate this phase of life, it becomes crucial to foster resilience, adaptability, and acceptance. Connecting with support systems, including family, friends, and healthcare professionals, can provide valuable resources and encouragement during times of illness and aging.

By embracing a holistic approach to health and wellness that encompasses physical, mental, and emotional well-being, individuals can enhance their quality of life and navigate the transitions of aging and illness with grace and dignity. It's through these experiences that we gain insights, wisdom, and a deeper appreciation for the complexity and resilience of the human body and spirit.

Chapter Four

Suffering and happiness depend on your own actions.

This principle is central to the teachings of Buddhism and other philosophies. It suggests that the way we act and the decisions we make have a direct impact on our experiences of suffering and happiness. By taking responsibility for our actions and striving to act in positive, compassionate ways, we can cultivate happiness and reduce suffering in our lives. This concept emphasizes the importance of mindfulness, self-awareness, and ethical behavior in shaping our overall well-being.

It is important to understand that our actions, big or small, can have significant consequences on our well-being and the well-being of those around us. By cultivating qualities such as kindness, compassion, and mindfulness, we can create positive outcomes and reduce suffering in the world. Taking accountability for our actions and striving to make choices that align with our values and ethical principles can lead us towards greater happiness and fulfillment.

Moreover, the concept that suffering and happiness depend on our own actions also highlights the power of agency and free will in shaping our lives. Despite external circumstances and challenges, we have the capacity to choose how we respond and act in any given situation. This empowerment invites us to be proactive in creating the kind of life we desire, rather than feeling helpless or victimized by external forces.

In essence, understanding that suffering and happiness are influenced by our actions can be a transformative insight. It encourages us to reflect on the choices we make, the attitudes we hold, and the impact we have on ourselves and others. By embracing this principle, we can embark on a journey of self-discovery, growth, and ultimately, the pursuit of a more meaningful and fulfilling life.

This understanding emphasizes the interconnectedness of our actions and their consequences on both our own well-being and the well-being of those around us. It underscores the importance of cultivating positive qualities like kindness, compassion, and mindfulness to promote positive outcomes and reduce suffering in the world.

By acknowledging the influence of our choices on our happiness and the happiness of others, we are empowered to take accountability for our actions and make decisions that align with our values and ethical beliefs. This self-awareness and commitment to conscious decision-making can lead us toward greater fulfillment and satisfaction in our lives.

Furthermore, recognizing that our responses to challenges and circumstances shape our experiences highlights the power of agency and free will in influencing our well-being. Rather than feeling passively acted upon by external events, we can actively choose our responses and behaviors, ultimately shaping the direction of our lives.

By internalizing the idea that our actions play a significant role in determining our happiness and overall quality of life, we are prompted to reflect on our behaviors, beliefs, and impacts on the world around us. This awareness invites us to embark on a journey of personal growth, self-discovery, and the pursuit of a purposeful and fulfilling life filled with meaning and positive impact.

Reflecting on the interconnectedness of our actions and their consequences also fosters a sense of responsibility towards the greater good. It prompts us to consider the ripple effects of our choices on the world at large, encouraging us to act with kindness, empathy, and integrity in all interactions. By recognizing the impact, we have on others through our actions, we become more mindful of how our behaviors can contribute to either positive or negative outcomes in society.

Moreover, the principle that suffering and happiness are influenced by our actions invites us to engage in ongoing self-examination and personal growth. It challenges us to confront our biases, assumptions, and habits that may be hindering our well-being and potential for happiness. Through this introspective journey, we have the opportunity to cultivate greater self-awareness, emotional intelligence, and resilience in the face of life's challenges.

Taking ownership of our actions and their impact on our well-being and that of others can also lead to a deeper sense of fulfillment and satisfaction. When we align our behaviors with our core values and principles, we experience a greater sense of integrity and authenticity in how we navigate the world. This alignment fosters a stronger sense of purpose and meaning in our lives, as we actively contribute to the well-being of ourselves and those around us.

In essence, understanding the profound influence of our actions on our happiness and the happiness of others serves as a powerful reminder of the interconnected nature of human existence. By embracing this awareness and committing to intentional, values-driven living, we can collectively create a more compassionate, harmonious, and fulfilling world for all beings.

Living in alignment with our values and principles allows us to cultivate a mutual respect for ourselves and others, fostering healthy and positive relationships. By taking responsibility for our actions and their consequences, we can strive to make choices that benefit not only ourselves but also our communities and the world at large.

Furthermore, this mindful approach to living empowers us to recognize the ripple effect of our actions and how they contribute to the greater good. It encourages us to practice kindness, empathy, and understanding in our interactions, promoting a culture of compassion and cooperation.

Ultimately, by consciously acknowledging the impact of our choices on our well-being and the well-being of others, we can create a more empathetic and interconnected world where individuals thrive in harmony and unity. Through our commitment to living authentically and in alignment with our values, we can each play a part in shaping a better future for ourselves and generations to come.

Living authentically and in alignment with our values also strengthens our sense of self-awareness and emotional well-being Living authentically and in line with our values also allows us to foster a deeper sense of self-awareness and personal growth. When we hold ourselves accountable for our actions and their effects on both ourselves and others, we open ourselves up to valuable opportunities for reflection, learning, and improvement.

By staying true to our core values and principles, we build a strong foundation that guides our decisions and behaviors in a way that is congruent with our true selves. This authenticity can lead to a greater sense of inner peace, confidence, and fulfillment as we navigate life's challenges with integrity and purpose.

Moreover, when we prioritize values-driven living, we inspire and influence those around us to do the same. Our actions serve as a model for others to follow, creating a positive ripple effect that extends beyond ourselves and into our communities and beyond.

In essence, embracing the interconnected nature of our actions and their impact on our well-being and the well-being of others can empower us to lead more meaningful, purposeful lives filled with compassion, empathy, and authenticity. It is through this conscious awareness and commitment to values-driven living that we can collectively contribute to a more harmonious, compassionate, and fulfilling world for all.

In the past we have discussed the nature of living things and non-living things, that they have already come into existence. existed for a while according to their lifespan and finally disappeared from this world. It is the decay or death itself. And this fourth chapter will talk about Our human actions while we are alive. It will be happy and how much suffering is there?

The truth is what can be done in your life, it is up to us, it is the highest truth. It sounds like discussing the nature of existence and the choices we make as humans during our lifetimes. It's true that living things have a lifespan and eventually come to an end through decay or death. The way we live our lives, the actions we take, and the impact we have on others can determine whether we find happiness or suffering. Ultimately, it is up to us to choose our path and create our reality. Our actions and decisions shape our experiences and the world around us.

Our actions carry weight beyond our individual lives, influencing the experiences of those around us and shaping the world for future generations. Whether it's through acts of kindness, compassion, creativity, or simply being present for others, each choice we make ripples out into the world in ways we may not always fully grasp.

While the impermanence of life is a universal truth, the opportunity to bring joy, meaning, and positive change to ourselves and others is also ever-present. The awareness of our own mortality can serve as a reminder to live fully, authentically, and in alignment with our values and aspirations.

In navigating the complexities of existence, we can find solace in the agency we hold to create moments of beauty, connection, growth, and transformation. By embracing the highest truth of our potential for compassion, empathy, and love, we can strive to leave a legacy of kindness and light in a world that is often marked by impermanence and uncertainty.

Indeed, embracing the impermanence of life can motivate us to cherish each moment, deepen our relationships, and pursue our passions with vigor. By recognizing the fragility of our existence, we can cultivate gratitude for the experiences and connections that enrich our lives.

Through acts of kindness, generosity, and understanding, we can leave a positive impact that endures beyond our time here. By choosing to live authentically and with purpose, we can contribute to a more compassionate and interconnected world, transcending the boundaries of mortality.

In the face of life's uncertainties, our capacity to create beauty, meaning, and joy shines brightly as a beacon of hope and resilience. Let us honor the impermanence of life by living with intention, savoring each moment, and spreading love in all that we do to embrace the full spectrum of human experience, acknowledging that within the impermanence lies the opportunity for growth, renewal, and transformation. Our mortality serves as a poignant reminder to live with intention, to cultivate our inner resources of strength and resilience, and to foster a sense of connection with ourselves and others.

As we navigate the ebb and flow of life's complexities, we are called to cultivate a spirit of curiosity, openness, and acceptance. By leaning into the inherent impermanence of all things, we can uncover hidden depths of wisdom, compassion, and grace. Our willingness to engage with life's transience can lead us to a profound understanding of our interconnectedness with all beings and the natural world.

In each moment, we have the opportunity to sow seeds of kindness, empathy, and understanding, knowing that our actions ripple outwards in ways both seen and unseen. By embracing our mortality as a catalyst for living authentically and with purpose, we can transcend our individual fears and limitations, and tap into a deeper wellspring of courage and creativity.

Let us embrace the impermanence of life as a sacred dance between light and shadow, joy and sorrow, birth and death. In the tapestry of existence, may we find solace in the impermanent nature of all things, and in doing so, discover the timeless truth of our interconnectedness and shared humanity.

Life cannot choose to be born. But you can choose to behave yourself as a good person.

Our own actions are the product of our family upbringing and ancestors. If we are in a good environment but do bad things, there are too many bad things. And if there are people who are born in an environment that is not perfect and are not ready. But he is a good person because he is a person who can choose to determine the direction of his own life. and have determination to live life and not abandon opportunities

despite challenging circumstances. While our upbringing and ancestral influences may shape our initial inclinations and perspectives, we possess the power to make choices and take actions that can diverge from the paths set by our past. Through determination and a strong will to live a fulfilling life, individuals can overcome adversity, seize opportunities, and chart their own course. Ultimately, our capacity to make decisions and shape our destinies demonstrates the resilience and autonomy inherent in the human spirit.

Certainly! Even when faced with difficult environments or unfavorable circumstances, individuals have the ability to exercise their agency and make conscious decisions that lead to positive outcomes. It is through the strength of our character, the resilience of our spirit, and the power of our choices that we can transcend the limitations imposed by our past. By embracing opportunities and demonstrating a commitment to personal growth and self-improvement, we can steer our lives in a direction aligned with our values and aspirations. Through perseverance and a steadfast determination to overcome obstacles, we can forge our own path and create a future defined by hope, resilience, and a sense of purpose.

That's a thoughtful perspective. While we may not have control over our beginning, we do have the power to shape our actions and make positive choices throughout our lives. Being a good person is a choice we can make every day through our words, actions, and interactions with others.

Life's journey may not always be in our hands, but how we navigate it and the impact we leave on the world and those around us is within our control. Our choices, attitudes, and behaviors influence the legacy we create and the mark we leave behind. Embracing kindness, empathy, and integrity can transform not only our own lives but also the lives of others. So, let's strive to be the architects of our character, crafting a story of compassion, understanding, and positivity in the tapestry of existence.

Good action to create good happy

Any action that creates happiness that does not cause other people to suffer and does not interfere with happiness or cause other people to suffer, that action will make you all happy and eternally happy. Not causing other people to have pain caused by our actions is a good thing that will carry with us until we die. These things are about knowing how to be merciful, how to forgive, how to respect the rights of other people, how to lose, how to forgive, how to know. Recognize and see what should be reasonable and always be mindful in any action in life without causing negligence.

Indeed, promoting happiness while ensuring that our actions do not impede the happiness of others is a fundamental principle for leading a fulfilling and harmonious life. Demonstrating mercy, forgiveness, respect for others' rights, and understanding in our interactions are crucial components of fostering positive relationships and contributing to a peaceful environment. Being mindful of our actions and their potential impacts on others helps us navigate life with greater awareness and empathy. Following these principles can lead to a more compassionate and fulfilling existence for all.

Also Here are some additional thoughts on the importance of compassion, empathy, and mindfulness in our daily interactions:

Practicing kindness and compassion towards others not only benefits them but also enriches our own lives. When we approach situations with empathy and understanding, we cultivate deeper connections with those around us and create a positive ripple effect in our communities.

Forgiveness is a powerful tool that liberates us from the burden of holding onto grudges and resentment. By learning to forgive, we free ourselves from negative emotions and create space for healing and growth, both for ourselves and for those we forgive.

Respecting the rights and dignity of others is essential for fostering a sense of mutual respect and cooperation in society. When we acknowledge the value and worth of every individual, we contribute to building a more inclusive and harmonious world.

Learning how to gracefully handle loss and setbacks is a valuable skill that teaches us resilience and strength. By embracing challenges with a resilient spirit, we grow and evolve, gaining wisdom and maturity along the way.

Being mindful of our actions means being fully present in the moment and considering the consequences of our choices. By cultivating mindfulness, we develop a heightened sense of awareness that allows us to make decisions that align with our values and intentions.

Ultimately, by embodying these principles of mercy, forgiveness, respect, resilience, and mindfulness in our daily lives, we can create a more compassionate, harmonious, and fulfilling existence for ourselves and those around us.

Practicing mindfulness can help us foster a deep connection with our surroundings, improve our relationships, and promote emotional well-being. By being fully present and aware of our actions, we can approach challenges with clarity and compassion, leading to more positive outcomes for ourselves and others. Cultivating mindfulness allows us to respond thoughtfully rather than reacting impulsively, fostering a sense of inner peace and balance in our lives.

To cultivate mindfulness can also enhance our overall mental clarity and focus. By training our minds to be present and attentive, we can improve our ability to concentrate on tasks, leading to increased productivity and effectiveness in our daily activities.

In addition, practicing mindfulness can help us manage stress and anxiety more effectively. By being fully aware of our thoughts and emotions in the present moment, we can develop better coping mechanisms for handling challenging situations and reducing mental clutter. This heightened self-awareness enables us to approach difficulties with a sense of calm and resilience, allowing us to navigate life's ups and downs with greater ease.

Moreover, mindfulness can deepen our connections with others and enrich our relationships. By being fully present in our interactions, we can listen more attentively, communicate more effectively, and show genuine empathy and compassion towards those around us. This fosters positive and meaningful connections with others, leading to more harmonious and fulfilling relationships in both our personal and professional lives.

Embracing mindfulness as a way of life can ultimately lead to a more authentic and purposeful existence. By aligning our actions with our values and intentions, we can live a life guided by compassion, understanding, and inner peace. Through the practice of mindfulness, we can create a ripple effect of positivity and harmony that extends not only to ourselves but also to the world around us.

Summary of this book

In this book, the author hopes that readers will receive the greatest benefits and eternal truths about the cycle of life and the cycle of birth, existence and destruction. Life that results from aging or death leaves this world. These processes are processes from beginning to end. The duration may not be the same. Some living things may have very short lives, some non-living things may It has a lifespan according to the lifespan of the object, and it is the true truth of all human beings and wild animals in this world.

The author delves into the interconnected themes of life and death, emphasizing how these processes are universal and inevitable. With a focus on the cyclical nature of existence, the book aims to impart profound insights into the transient essence of life and the natural course of birth, growth, decay, and death. By exploring the varying durations of life across different organisms and objects, the author highlights the fundamental truth that all living beings, including humans and wild animals, are bound by these inherent cycles. Through these reflections, readers are encouraged to contemplate the deeper meanings surrounding mortality, impermanence, and the enduring legacy of existence.

Reflecting on the interconnected themes of life and death, the author invites readers to contemplate the profound implications of the cyclical nature of existence. By delving into the eternal truths regarding birth, growth, decay, and mortality, the book offers a unique perspective on the universal processes that govern all living beings. Through poignant narratives and insightful reflections, the author sheds light on the transient essence of life and the inherent fragility of existence. By exploring the diverse lifespans of various organisms and objects, the book underscores the fundamental reality that all beings are subject to the immutable laws of nature. In illuminating the intricate tapestry of life's ebbs and flows, the author hopes to inspire readers to embrace the beauty and impermanence of every moment, recognizing the profound significance of the cycle of life in all its complexity.

The author's exploration of the interconnected themes of life and death encourages readers to engage in deep contemplation about the fundamental aspects of existence. Through the lens of the cyclical nature of life, readers are prompted to reflect on the inevitability of change, transformation, and eventual decay that all living entities experience. By weaving together narratives that touch upon the interconnectedness of all living beings and the transient nature of life, the author underscores the universal truths that bind all forms of life together.

The book's poignant reflections on the fragility of existence prompt readers to appreciate the beauty and impermanence of life's moments. By examining the diverse lifespans of various organisms and objects, the author emphasizes the underlying unity in the shared experience of birth, growth, and eventual decline. Through this exploration, readers are invited to acknowledge the profound significance of each fleeting moment and embrace the inherent cycles that shape the tapestry of life.

In shedding light on the intricate tapestry of life's ebbs and flows, the author aims to inspire readers to find meaning in the complexities and uncertainties of existence. By recognizing the transformative power of the cycle of life, readers are encouraged to cherish the present moment and find solace in the interconnectedness of all living beings. Ultimately, the book serves as a reminder of the cyclical nature of life and offers a lens through which readers can cultivate a deeper understanding of the universal processes that govern the essence of existence.

Exploring the profound implications of life and death through various perspectives and narratives, the author challenges readers to confront their own mortality and consider the interconnectedness of all living beings. By delving into the complexities of birth, growth, decay, and mortality, the book invites readers to grapple with the inherent fragility and preciousness of life itself. Through a juxtaposition of stark realities and poetic reflections, the author illuminates the beauty found in the impermanence of existence, urging readers to embrace the fleeting nature of every moment.

As the narratives unfold, showcasing the diverse lifespans of organisms and objects, a sense of interconnectedness emerges—a recognition of the shared experience of growth and eventual decline that binds all living beings together. Through these poignant explorations, the author highlights the cyclical nature of existence, offering a profound meditation on the essence of life and the universal laws that govern all living things.

In contemplating the intricate tapestry of life's ebbs and flows, readers are encouraged to find meaning in the transient nature of existence and to seek solace in the rhythms that shape the world around them. By delving into the depths of the cycle of life, the author hopes to awaken a sense of wonder and gratitude for the time-bound journey that each individual embarks upon. Through this reflection on life's interconnected themes, readers are invited to embrace the beauty and impermanence of every moment, recognizing the profound significance of the cycle of life in shaping their understanding of the world and their place within it.

The author's exploration of the interconnectedness of all beings and objects serves as a powerful reminder of the universal truths that govern life's unfolding. Through contemplation of growth, decay, and renewal, readers are invited to reflect on their own place within the larger tapestry of existence. The cyclical nature of life, with its inherent rhythms of birth and death, offers a lens through which to view the world with greater depth and appreciation.

By weaving together narratives that span different lifespans and experiences, the author invites readers to embrace the impermanence of all things and find beauty in the continuous cycle of creation and dissolution. This meditation on the essence of life encourages a sense of interconnectedness and unity among all living beings, fostering a deeper understanding of the intrinsic bonds that tie us together.

Ultimately, the author's poignant reflections on the cycle of life serve as a poignant reminder of the profound interconnectedness of all beings and the sacredness of each moment in our shared journey through existence. Through this exploration, readers are called to embrace the ebb and flow of life's rhythms, finding solace and inspiration in the timeless dance of growth and decay that shapes our world.

The author skillfully weaves a tapestry of interconnected stories that highlight the intricate web of life, showcasing how each individual thread contributes to the larger design. Through the lens of various characters and their evolving narratives, readers are encouraged to contemplate the transient nature of existence and the profound beauty that emerges from the constant flux of creation and destruction.

In delving into the universal themes of impermanence and interconnectedness, the author guides readers towards a deeper appreciation for the intricate balance that sustains all life forms. By depicting the cyclical nature of birth, growth, death, and rebirth, the narrative underscores the interconnectedness of all living beings and the interwoven tapestry of existence that unites us all.

As readers immerse themselves in the author's reflections on the ephemerality of life, they are prompted to reflect on their own place within the vast cosmic tapestry, recognizing the intricate connections that bind us to each other and to the world at large. Through this exploration, the author invites us to embrace the profound wisdom that emerges from acknowledging the transient nature of all things and finding solace in the eternal rhythms that govern our shared journey through life.

The author's nuanced exploration of life's ephemeral nature challenges readers to confront their own relationship with impermanence and change, inviting them to consider the interconnectedness of all beings in the grand tapestry of existence. By intertwining diverse narratives that span generations and experiences, the author evokes a sense of shared humanity and interconnected destiny, resonating with readers on a deeply emotional level.

Through the intricate storytelling, the author not only celebrates the intricacies of life's cyclical rhythms but also underscores the transformative power of acceptance and interconnectedness. By embracing the beauty inherent in creation and dissolution, readers are invited to find meaning in the constant flux of existence and to discover a sense of unity that transcends individual experiences and lifetimes.

Ultimately, the author's profound meditation on the essence of life serves as a poignant reminder of the interconnected nature of all things, inspiring readers to seek solace in the eternal dance of growth and decay that shapes our world. In this exploration of the sacredness of existence, readers are encouraged to reflect on their own roles within the interconnected web of life, finding a renewed sense of purpose and interconnectedness in the universal journey that binds us all together.

Everything has its own agenda and everything in this world is impermanent. Don't be attached to it and use it as a public emotion. It will cause you more suffering than happiness.

This advice reflects a perspective from Buddhist teachings on impermanence and non-attachment. The idea is that everything in the world is subject to change and clinging to things, including emotions, can lead to suffering. By practicing non-attachment and accepting the impermanence of all things, one can find more peace and contentment in life.

Here's a continuation:

Practicing non-attachment does not necessarily mean avoiding emotions or experiences, but rather approaching them with a sense of equanimity and acceptance. By cultivating mindfulness and observing our thoughts and feelings without becoming consumed by them, we can develop a greater sense of inner peace and resilience.

In the face of life's ups and downs, recognizing the impermanence of all things can help us navigate challenges with a sense of grace and understanding. It reminds us that change is a natural part of life and that our attachment to outcomes can often lead to disappointment and suffering.

Ultimately, by letting go of our attachments and understanding the transient nature of all things, we can find a deeper sense of freedom and joy in the present moment. Embracing impermanence can be a profound practice that opens the door to greater wisdom, compassion, and inner strength.

Indeed, recognizing the impermanence of all things can be a powerful perspective to embrace. It teaches us to appreciate the present moment, let go of attachments, and navigate life's challenges with greater resilience. By understanding that change is inevitable and that nothing lasts forever, we can cultivate a more peaceful and balanced approach to life.

Embracing impermanence can also help us develop a sense of gratitude for the experiences and relationships we have in the here and now. It encourages us to savor each moment, knowing that it is unique and will not last forever. This mindfulness of impermanence can lead to a deeper appreciation of life and a more profound connection to the world around us.

By practicing acceptance of impermanence, we can learn to release our fears and anxieties about the future and instead focus on living fully in the present. This acceptance can bring us a sense of freedom and openness, allowing us to move through life with greater ease and authenticity. Ultimately, embracing impermanence can be a transformative practice that brings us closer to our true selves and helps us cultivate a deeper sense of peace and fulfillment.

Reflecting further on the concept of impermanence, we can see how it applies to various aspects of our lives. From the changing seasons to the growth and aging of living beings, impermanence is a fundamental aspect of the natural world. By recognizing this fundamental truth, we can learn to let go of our attachments and expectations, allowing us to flow more gracefully with the ever-changing currents of life.

Impermanence also teaches us the value of mindfulness and presence. When we are fully engaged in the present moment, we are better able to appreciate the beauty and richness of life as it unfolds before us. By embracing impermanence, we can learn to let go of regrets about the past and worries about the future, and instead focus on living with intention and purpose in the here and now.

Moreover, understanding impermanence can lead us to cultivate a greater sense of compassion and empathy for ourselves and others. When we recognize that everyone and everything is subject to change, we are more likely to approach others with kindness, understanding, and forgiveness. This shift in perspective can deepen our connections with those around us and foster a sense of unity and interconnectedness with all beings.

In essence, embracing impermanence is a transformative practice that can lead us to a more authentic, resilient, and fulfilling way of being. By living in harmony with the ever-changing nature of existence, we can discover a profound sense of freedom, joy, and peace that transcends the ups and downs of life. It is through this awareness and acceptance of impermanence that we can truly navigate life's challenges with grace and understanding, fostering a deeper sense of wisdom and inner strength along the way.

Embracing impermanence can help us cultivate a mindset that values the present moment and appreciates the beauty of life as it unfolds. It encourages us to let go of attachment to outcomes, release fear of change, and embrace the flow of life with an open heart. By acknowledging that everything is transient, we learn to cherish each experience and relationship more deeply, knowing that they are fleeting and precious.

This acceptance of impermanence also enables us to respond to setbacks and difficulties with greater resilience and perspective. Instead of resisting change or clinging to the past, we can adapt and grow through life's inevitable transitions. This adaptability fosters a sense of inner peace and contentment, knowing that we have the strength and flexibility to navigate whatever comes our way.

Ultimately, by embracing impermanence, we can find a profound sense of freedom and liberation from the constraints of fear and anxiety. We can live more fully in the present moment, savoring each experience and connection, and becoming more attuned to the beauty and wonder of life. This transformative practice can lead us to a more authentic, joyful, and fulfilling existence, enriching our lives with wisdom, compassion, and a deep sense of interconnectedness with all beings.

Embracing impermanence invites us to cultivate a deeper sense of mindfulness and presence in our daily lives. It encourages us to let go of rigid expectations and judgments, allowing us to approach each moment with curiosity and openness. By acknowledging the impermanent nature of all things, we can release the grip of attachment and learn to flow with the rhythms of life.

This practice of impermanence also reminds us of the interconnectedness of all beings and the interdependence of the world around us. When we embrace the transient nature of existence, we develop a greater sense of empathy, compassion, and gratitude for the people and experiences that enrich our lives. This awareness can lead to more meaningful relationships, a stronger sense of community, and a greater appreciation for the interconnected web of life.

Moreover, embracing impermanence can help us overcome the fear of failure, loss, or change. It allows us to approach challenges with a sense of curiosity and resilience, knowing that every experience, whether joyful or challenging, is an opportunity for growth and learning. By embracing impermanence, we can cultivate a sense of inner strength and courage that enables us to face life's uncertainties with grace and resilience.

In essence, embracing impermanence is a transformative practice that can enrich every aspect of our lives. It invites us to live with greater awareness, compassion, and resilience, helping us to navigate life's challenges with grace and wisdom. By developing a deeper understanding and acceptance of impermanence, we can cultivate a profound sense of freedom, joy, and peace that permeates every moment of our existence.

Live your life happily and
don't be careless.